The Cull

The Cull

Michele Riml and
Michael St. John Smith

The Cull
first published 2025 by Scirocco Drama
An imprint of J. Gordon Shillingford Publishing Inc.

Scirocco Drama Editor: Glenda MacFarlane
Cover design by Doowah Design
Photo of Michele Riml by Michael O'Shea.
Photo of Michael St. John Smith by Brandon Hart Photography
Production photos by Moonrider Productions for the Arts Club Theatre Company

Printed and bound in Canada on 100% post-consumer recycled paper.

Production inquiries to:
Marquis Literary, www.MQlit.ca
Colin Rivers / colin@MQent.ca

Library and Archives Canada Cataloguing in Publication

Title: The cull / Michele Riml & Michael St. John Smith.
Names: Riml, Michele, author. | Smith, Michael St. John, author.
Identifiers: Canadiana 20250259621 | ISBN 9781990738739 (softcover)
Subjects: LCGFT: Drama.
Classification: LCC PS8635.I555 C85 2025 | DDC C812/.6—dc23

We acknowledge the financial support of the Canada Council for the Arts, the Government of Canada, the Manitoba Arts Council, and the Manitoba Government for our publishing program.

J. Gordon Shillingford Publishing
P.O. Box 86, RPO Corydon Avenue, Winnipeg, MB Canada R3M 3S3

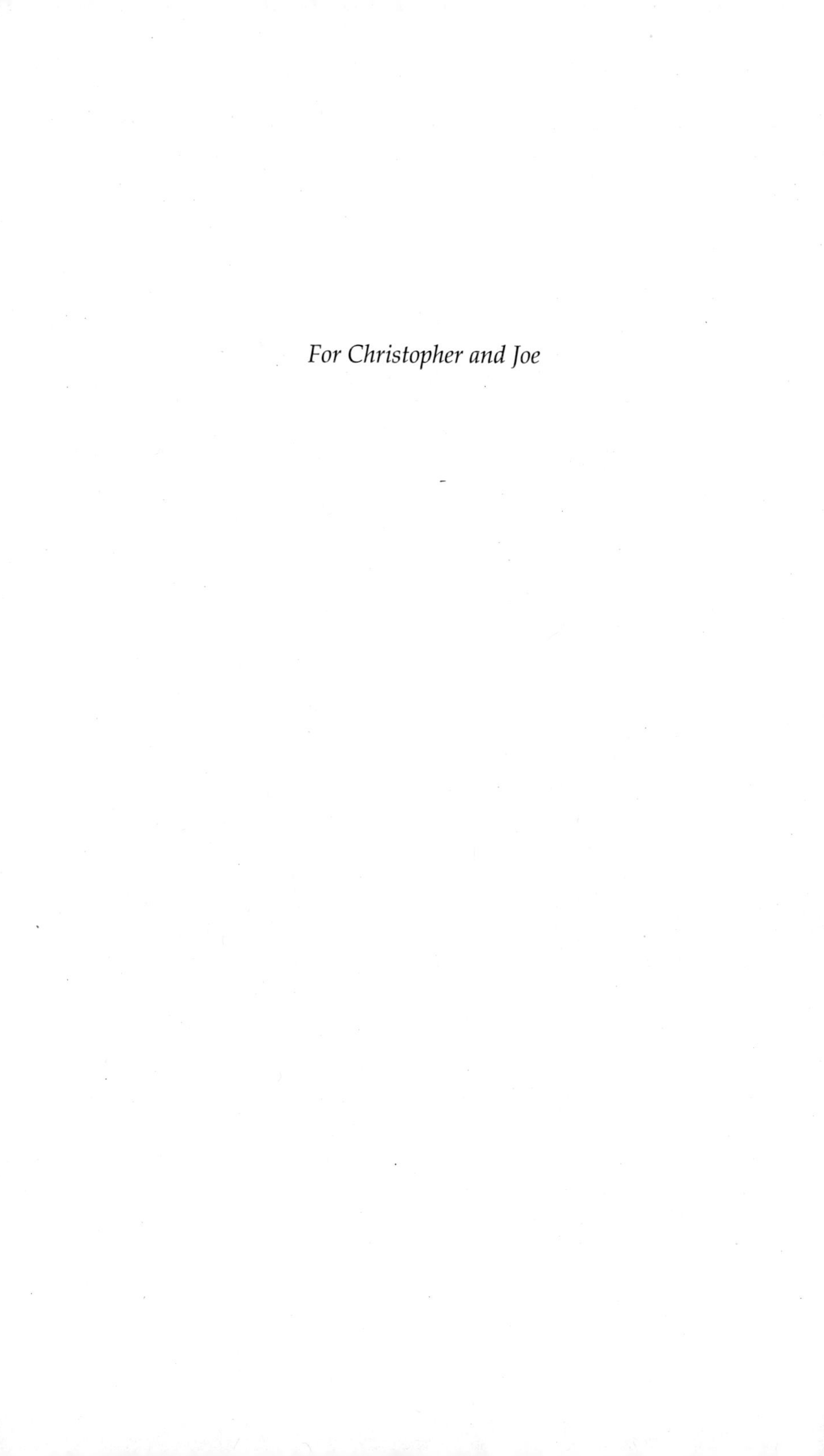

For Christopher and Joe

Michele Riml

Michele Riml is a critically acclaimed playwright from Vancouver, British Columbia. Michele's first play, *Souvenirs,* won The BC Young Playwrights Search. Some of her plays include *Under the Influence, Poster Boys, RAGE,* which won the 2005 Sydney Risk Award and has been produced in French, Polish and German, *On the Edge,* and *The Amaryllis,* which was produced by The Search Party and premiered at The Fire Hall Theatre in Vancouver in the fall of 2020. *The Cull,* co-written with Michael St. John Smith, premiered at The Arts Club Theatre in 2023.

Michele's play *Sexy Laundry* has been translated into more than fifteen languages, and has ongoing productions in Canada, the United States and Europe, along with its sequel *Henry and Alice: Into the Wild.*

Michele is also a writer for young audiences, and her YPT plays have been widely produced and translated. They include *The Skinny Lie, The Invisible Girl* and *Tree Boy,* published by National Geographic and most recently produced in Athens, Greece. Her most recent play, *She Shoots, She Scores!,* an adaptation of hockey legend Cammi Granato's book *I Can Play, Too!,* will premiere in 2026 with Green Thumb Theatre.

Michele Riml is an FPA graduate from Simon Fraser University. In 2008, she was nominated for the Siminovitch Prize.

Michael St. John Smith

Michael St. John Smith is a writer, film actor and screenwriting instructor. Michael has authored four stage plays, including the Jessie-nominated *Slaying Dragons*, *The Biz* and *The Bridge* (co-written with Michele Riml for Pi Theatre and produced as a CBC podcast.) His fourth play, *The Cull* (co-written with Michele Riml,) premiered at the Arts Club in January of 2023.

Michael has also written several commissioned screenplays. These include an adaptation of the Ivan Coyote novel *Bow Grip* with Telefilm Canada, *The Pen and the Sword*, an animated TV pilot for Devine Entertainment, and most recently, *Archangel*, an original sci-fi feature co-written with *New York Times* best-selling author, William Gibson, with support from the Harold Greenberg Fund. *Archangel* was adapted as a graphic novel and is currently being developed as a TV series with Copperheart Entertainment.

Michael St. John Smith graduated from Harvard University with honours in English Literature.

Acknowledgements

The playwrights would like to acknowledge and thank:

Stephen Drover, dramaturg, for his many, many careful readings of the play and his thoughtful contributions to the script; Ashlie Corcoran, Artistic Director of the Arts Club Theatre Company; Stan and Kathy Hamilton (Silver Commission, Arts Club); Rachel Ditor; and Bill Millard (Artistic Director Emeritus, Arts Club Theatre Company).

Mark Strongman for The Meat. And Arthur Patterson for the Wine.

Darcy Peel for the wolf cull conversation.

Brad Assu, for sharing his knowledge about Kwakiutl mask carving and Indigenous culture.

The original cast, crew, and production team at the Arts Club Theatre Company, for keeping the faith—and the fire—alive through the pandemic, and for creating a powerful first production of *The Cull*.

Ted Dykstra and Peter Pasyk, for their valuable notes and insight into the script.

And Colin Rivers, agent and friend, for his unwavering support of this play from the very beginning.

Foreword

When I was in Grade Two, a kid in my class said to me during recess, "If you give me that fruit roll-up, I'll be your friend." Of course, I gave it to him because who doesn't want a friend? Especially when that friend was a "cool kid." After a rather concise companionship, he wandered off (I suppose a fruit roll-up is only worth about forty-five minutes). I felt pretty confused at the time, but watching him walk away, I *did* know that I'd made a bad deal.

Many years later, when I read the first draft of the first act of *The Cull,* I thought, "There is something very familiar about this." Like the character Emily in the play, there have been times when I've felt like I was on the periphery of a friend group: ostensibly a member of the Cool Kids' Club but also running to keep up and working harder than I want to. Invariably, I end up wondering, "Is this friendship worth this many fruit roll-ups?" While reading Michele and Michael's remarkable script, I began to see this idea of the deals we make to get what we want explored in a larger, more adult context.

The play introduces us to a group of old friends, most of whom have money: they've been on expensive vacations, they have a $20,000 chandelier and a walk-in humidor, they own "nice things." They have stuff they enjoy, and they like to show it off. Set within this group are the more modest Emily and Lewis who have watched their childhood friend group over the years gradually reinvent itself as successful and comfortable while they struggle to make ends meet and work to stick with (or are stuck with) their values of sustainability, a relationship to the land, and simple living. When the promise of comfort and security are waved in front of them, they are tempted with the possibility of seeing their problems seemingly dissolve by simply reaching out and taking a cheque. They choose to make that deal with the excuse that you "gotta grow up sometime."

As the evening evolves, the question of whether they can stomach the deal becomes the drumbeat of the play. What begins as a well-intentioned celebration soon spirals into a night of moral reckoning. Relationships are tested, alliances shift, and as the stakes escalate, perhaps we—the audience—begin to consider the consequences of our *own* priorities and what we may be sacrificing to achieve them. The commodification of friendship, so prevalent in the schoolyard, sometimes follows us into adulthood (the fruit roll-ups just get more expensive), and sometimes, under the persuasive guise of "just doing business," we forget what's important. *The Cull*, then, becomes a sort of cautionary tale informed by materialist thinking, peer pressure, and how we reinvent our past in the name of "nostalgia."

Wonderfully, nestled in this narrative is a very familiar and contemporary debate about what "doing the right thing" looks like and how at times our good intentions have limits. Lynn's plan to turn her family orchard into an eco-tourism destination is wrapped in her story of preserving nature and sharing a magical place with people—even though it will cost guests—and most likely the environment— a premium price. John asserts that making seemingly ethical choices like recycling, buying local, and protecting the environment are simply a sort of karmic currency that makes us feel better about having more stuff. While I don't want to agree with him, it's a troubling theory. Maybe I'll feel better about driving my gas-powered car if I choose paper straws…??

By inserting this debate into the story, *The Cull* encourages us to broaden our understanding of how so many aspects of our world can be commodified: property, friendship, even ethics. *Why should we "do the right thing" when the rewards of moral compromise appear to be far more tangible, immediate, and satisfying?* The play confronts us with difficult questions like this yet offers no answers, instead encouraging us to continue the debate long after we've seen or read it.

The Cull strikingly reminds us that, despite having primal instincts and desires, we also always have a choice. It counters materialist cynicism with an investment in hope: if we find ourselves in a bad deal, it might not be too late to back out and take stock of what we *already* have. Perhaps we don't really need (or, on deeper evaluation, *even want*) to own the shiniest new car, or have a walk-in humidor, or be one of the "cool kids." Perhaps the price of one's own integrity, sometimes in the innocent form of a fruit roll-up, is ultimately just too high. Maybe, in the end, all we really need is each other, some breathing space, and a clear, open night sky under which we can share our own hard-won values, needs, and dreams.

Stephen Drover
June 2025

Stephen Drover is a dramaturg and director. He was born in Newfoundland, lives in Vancouver, and is the Head of New Works and Professional Engagement at the Arts Club Theatre Company. Stephen was the dramaturg for The Cull.

Production History

The Cull was originally produced by the Arts Club Theatre Company (a Silver Commission,) at the Granville Island Stage in Vancouver, BC. It ran from January 26 to February 26, 2023, with the following cast and creative team:

Cast

Emily Casillo: ....Dawn Petten
Lewis Casillo: .... Stephen Lobo
Paul Rayburn: .... Craig Erickson
Nicole Rayburn: ....Meghan Gardiner
John Atkinson: ....John Cassini
Lynne Yu: .... Jasmine Chen

Creative Team

Playwrights: ....Michele Riml &
Michael St. John Smith
Director: ....Mindy Parfitt
Dramaturg: ....Stephen Drover
Set Designer: ....Amir Ofek
Costume Designer: ....Alaia Hamer
Lighting Designer: ....Ted Roberts
Sound Designer: ....Owen Belton
Intimacy Director: .... Phay Moores
Fight Director: .... Mike Kovac
Stage Manager: ....Rebecca Mulvihill
Assistant Stage Manager: ..... Marijka Asbeek Brusse

Note: *The Cull* was originally scheduled for production in 2020 but postponed due to Covid. It premiered as an audio play in November 2021 before its full stage debut.

Nicole (Meghan Gardiner) tells Emily (Dawn Petten) about her trip to Mexico. Photograph by Moonrider Productions for the Arts Club Theatre Company.

Lynne (Jasmine Chen) satisfies her hunger after dinner. Photograph by Moonrider Productions for the Arts Club Theatre Company.

Paul (Craig Erickson) and Lewis (Stephen Lobo) talk about the deal. In the background left to right: John (John Cassini), Lynne (Jasmine Chen), Nicole (Meghan Gardiner) and Emily (Dawn Petten). Photograph by Moonrider Productions for the Arts Club Theatre Company.

Nicole (Meghan Gardiner) serves her husband a piece of cake. Left to right: John (John Cassini), Lynne (Jasmine Chen), Lewis (Stephen Lobo), Emily (Dawn Petten), Paul (Craig Erickson). Photograph by Moonrider Productions for the Arts Club Theatre Company.

Nicole (Meghan Gardiner) and Paul (Craig Erickson) fight in their kitchen. Photograph by Moonrider Productions for the Arts Club Theatre Company.

Nicole (Meghan Gardiner) and Lewis (Stephen Lobo) have an intimate moment on the terrace. Photograph by Moonrider Productions for the Arts Club Theatre Company.

John (John Cassini) humiliates Paul (Craig Erickson). Left to right: Emily (Dawn Petten), Nicole (Meghan Gardiner), Lynne (Jasmine Chen), and Lewis (Stephen Lobo). Photograph by Moonrider Productions for the Arts Club Theatre Company.

Emily (Dawn Petten) and Lewis (Stephen Lobo) escape the party to admire the moon. Photograph by Moonrider Productions for the Arts Club Theatre Company.

The Characters

EMILY CASILLO	42 years old
LEWIS CASILLO	43 years old, married to Emily
NICOLE RAYBURN	39 years old
PAUL RAYBURN	43 years old, married to Nicole
LYNNE YU	43 years old
JOHN ATKINSON	61 years old, married to Lynne

The Setting

The play takes place in a nearly finished, custom-built post and beam home somewhere in the Interior of British Columbia. The set may be suggestive rather than literal, using a few key furnishings or abstract natural elements to evoke an open-plan kitchen and dining area, adjoining living room, den and outside terrace.

Key furnishings include a white couch and a large, expensive chandelier hanging over a hand-crafted cedar table. A Kwakiutl wolf mask, positioned in the living room, may be located on the fourth wall—indicated, but not seen. A large platter of raw beef sits covered on the table or counter.

It is eight o'clock in the evening in late July—still light outside. The hazy, reddish glow from a distant forest fire lingers throughout the play, deepening as night falls.

Note: It is the playwrights' intention to leave room for the director's interpretation of the set. The design may be as minimal or detailed as feels right to fully tell the story, using all or just a few of the suggested elements and props. That said, certain key moments require illumination—moments that call for physical action or specific objects. Real salad does not need to be chopped. But cake must be thrown. Red paint must be spilled. And the plate of raw meat—a visual anchor—is central to the play.

Scene One: Kitchen

The hazy reddish glow of a distant forest fire filters in through a window of PAUL and NICOLE's custom-built post and beam home.

NICOLE chops vegetables for a salad. EMILY scoops jelly onto cheese and crackers. They both drink white wine. A large platter of meat sits covered on the counter.

NICOLE: The thing about Mexico is...I'd love to just take my book and sit by the pool all day. But the kids—

EMILY: Get antsy, right?

NICOLE: You know, Em, they can't sit. And then there's Paul—

EMILY: —who's like a kid—

NICOLE: —who's worse than a kid! Jet skiing, ATVing— It's like if we're not doing something loud with a motor on it, it's not fun.

EMILY: You ATVed?

NICOLE: I burned it up. The kids loved it.

EMILY: Did Lynne and John go with you?

NICOLE throws her a look.

Work?

NICOLE: Her phone was blowing up the whole time. And John just disappears into his office all day... a whole floor of the house, overlooking the ocean. With a gym. Lucky guy.

EMILY: So their place is finished?

NICOLE: You know Lynne, it's never finished. But it's gorgeous. Lots of big linen sofas and cushions.

EMILY: She's really into natural fibres.

EMILY bites into a cracker and drops jelly on her dress.

Shoot! Well, I'm glad we could find a night that worked for everyone—

EMILY rubs at her dress, then arranges it to cover the stain. She looks at the chandelier hanging over the dining room table.

I love your new light. I saw something like it at Home Sense.

NICOLE: Thanks.

EMILY: You know, I'd really like to go back to Mexico one day. See that place with the beautiful arch. The one on your Facebook page.

NICOLE: El Arco.

EMILY goes back to the jelly, pushes the plate away.

EMILY: Beautiful. Oh my God! What is this stuff? It's dangerous.

NICOLE: Quince jelly. My mother's recipe.

EMILY: Let me make you one.

NICOLE: Not for me. Gotta watch the carbs.

EMILY: Training again?

NICOLE: Just a half-marathon. I've felt a little out of sync since Mexico. I'm hoping this'll get me going again— Ow!

NICOLE cuts her finger with the knife. EMILY jumps up.

EMILY: Are you okay?

NICOLE: It's fine— Fuck. How did I—

EMILY: You're bleeding. Band-aids are—?

NICOLE points at a drawer.

Sit. Let me see. Well... I think we can save the finger.

NICOLE: Stop it. I'm such a wuss.

EMILY tends to the cut.

You know, that was actually kind of a weird day. At El Arco.

EMILY: What do you mean?

NICOLE: I mean, it was beautiful. You take these little boats out there, and they drop you right on the beach. Pangas... that's what they call them. They bring a lot of tourists over. The locals love it, too. But there's plenty of room. Lizards and iguanas running all over the place.

EMILY: Keep your finger up.

NICOLE: The kids loved it. Paul played Frisbee with Sam and Sierra. I actually got to read my book. We swam. Had a picnic. Lynne brought this incredible picnic—

EMILY: Lynne and John came too?

NICOLE: Yeah, the whole pack. It was a beautiful day, right up to the end... 'til we had to leave. You know how John can be sometimes.

EMILY: "Time to GO!" You guys didn't want to leave?

NICOLE: Actually, we did. Sierra had a pretty bad sunburn.

EMILY: That fair skin...

NICOLE: I wanted to get them back to the condo. Lynne and John were walking on the beach. So Paul and I packed up our stuff and went down to where you catch the boat back to Cabo. Except there was this huge line, maybe sixty people waiting on the beach... and the boats only take about twelve people, right? Plus, it's Mexico so you don't know if the next boat is coming in fifteen minutes or an hour.

EMILY: Okay...

NICOLE: Well, anyway... I get in line with the kids and Paul goes off to find Lynne and John. Sierra and Sam start to fight about some shell he found and I'm trying to deal with it, and then I hear Paul yelling for me. He's at the head of the lineup and John—somehow John is already on the boat talking to the Mexican driver guy. I see John give him something and the driver goes over to a group of locals sitting in the back, and next thing, they're all getting off the boat—

EMILY: What?

NICOLE: I know. John and Paul are waving for us to come down. And I'm not sure what to do... the boat's totally full. All these people in line are looking at me— Next thing I know, Paul and Lynne are climbing on, and Paul's yelling, "Come on!"

EMILY: They had to get off the boat?

NICOLE: What?

EMILY: The Mexicans?

NICOLE: Two teenaged girls, an old man, and a couple with a toddler.

EMILY: Oh my God. What did you do?

NICOLE: Me? I... I got on the boat. What could I do? The kids were... Paul was yelling for us. We were holding everyone up.

EMILY: They kicked those people off the boat to make room for you?

NICOLE: Yes. It was very uncomfortable. I think John gave them some money.

EMILY: You said he paid the driver.

NICOLE: Yes, but the driver must have looked after them.

EMILY: Did you say something to John?

NICOLE: No, but Paul and I got into a huge argument, later.

EMILY: But what about John?

NICOLE: Well, I'm sure he knew how I felt. And I didn't go out for dinner with them that night. Paul went without me.

EMILY: I couldn't do that. No way.

NICOLE: Well, you don't know until you're there. John can be very—

EMILY: No, I'm sorry. I know you're not like that.

NICOLE: It happened so fast.

EMILY: Of course it did.

Voices from offstage as LEWIS and PAUL enter.

NICOLE:	Anyway. Enough of that. Drink up. This is your night.	PAUL:	*(Offstage.)* So the guy's like sure, retrofit the cabinetry, nothing custom. In and out. And then I get his invoice. Fuck me. You'd think he built the Taj Mahal. Plus he did a shitty job...

LEWIS: How many units?

PAUL: Thirteen. You'll be done in a week.

PAUL grabs the bottle and fills the women's glasses.

EMILY: I need to pace myself. Wait 'til everybody's here.

PAUL: *(To EMILY.)* What? No pacing, woman. This is your party!

PAUL slices himself a huge piece of cheese, slathers it with jelly, and eats it in a single bite.

NICOLE: So, what did you think, Lewis? Of the new addition to Paul's den? Ridiculous, right?

LEWIS: Pretty sweet.

NICOLE: Traitor.

PAUL: See? Lewis appreciates the need.

PAUL makes another cracker.

NICOLE: Nobody *needs* a temperature-controlled humidor bigger than my walk-in closet. Leave some cheese for Lynne and John!

PAUL: Wrong. A fine cigar needs a suitable home. And a man who appreciates a fine cigar needs a humidor.

He stuffs the cracker in his mouth, triumphantly.

NICOLE: There's a difference between needing and wanting something.

PAUL: —But what if I need you, *and* I want you!

PAUL embraces NICOLE and sniffs her neck.

PAUL: ...and now I have you! Jesus, you smell good. Is that the stuff I bought you?

NICOLE Stop it, you weirdo! Let me go.

PAUL: Hey, smell my wife, you two. She smells amazing.

NICOLE: Paul! I'm cooking.

PAUL: Come on, Em, have a sniff...

NICOLE holds out her wrist.

EMILY: Wow! It's beautiful. Where did you get it?

NICOLE: Lynne told me about this place in New York. Paul got it for me for Christmas.

PAUL: Come on, Lewis. Smell my wife. You know you want to...

NICOLE nods to LEWIS. He holds her wrist and sniffs.

LEWIS: Mint. Something citrus...

NICOLE: Lemon.

LEWIS: And... something flowery... geranium?

NICOLE: Good nose! PAUL: Geranium? What the— Who are you?

LEWIS: Smell is our strongest sense.

NICOLE: Do you like it?

LEWIS: I do.

PAUL: You know what it smells like to me? Money. Where are those two?

NICOLE: They'll be here.

PAUL: I'm glad he didn't try and fly up.

LEWIS: They wouldn't let him land. Airport's still closed. The fires.

EMILY: Are they staying with you?

NICOLE: Just for the night.

PAUL: So what do you think, man? Can you help me out with those *cabinets*?

LEWIS: I've got a small job on the Rez I'm finishing up—

NICOLE swats at them with a towel.

NICOLE: No! No business tonight, you guys. You know the rule, Paul. Where's your phone?

PAUL: This isn't business. I'm trying to put a few bucks in my best friend's pocket. I'm sure his wife won't mind.

LEWIS: We'd have to put off our camping trip—

EMILY: Take the job. I'll survive.

NICOLE takes a basket from the top of the fridge.

NICOLE: Paul. Phone.

PAUL: If Artie calls, I gotta take it—

NICOLE: Not tonight, you don't.

LEWIS: Nick's the boss.

EMILY: No technology for a night is a relief.

NICOLE: I just don't want tonight to be about business.

PAUL: But you do want a pool, right?

The doorbell rings. NICOLE grabs PAUL's phone from him as he leaves to get the door.

NICOLE: Not fair, Paul.

EMILY: You're getting a pool!

NICOLE: For the kids.

LEWIS: Fuck, what did I do with my phone? *(To EMILY.)* I think I lost my phone.

EMILY: You left it in the truck. We do this every day—

PAUL: *(Offstage.)* Hello, people! Good timing. They're ganging up on me here.

PAUL leads JOHN and LYNNE in. LYNNE carries a huge bouquet of flowers which she gives to EMILY.

JOHN is on his phone and carries a couple of bottles of red wine. Hugs and kisses and greetings all around.

NICOLE:	There they are!	LYNNE:	Oh my God, we made it! Hi!
EMILY:	We said no gifts!	JOHN:	*(On his phone.)* Well, figure something out and call him back. Or don't call him back. Let him sweat.

LYNNE: Not a gift, just flowers. Your hair, you changed it?

EMILY: I just blow-dried it. Special occasion.

LYNNE: Absolutely. You look beautiful, Em.

EMILY: Thank you.

LYNNE: John, c'mon!

JOHN: We don't need him. He needs us. Come at it that way, and it'll all work out. Got to go, I'm being rude. *(He hangs up.)* Hello! Sorry we're late. We drove like maniacs—

LYNNE: *You* drove like a maniac.

JOHN: Had to drive with the headlights on, you can't even see the sun...

LYNNE: Just this hazy orange glow. It was very creepy.

JOHN: Almost hit a fucking deer—

LYNNE: —Elk

JOHN: Elk... three of them darted out onto the highway maybe fifty feet in front of the car. I swerved to avoid 'em, went into a slide...

LYNNE: —you know how everything slows right down?

JOHN: —tires screeching...the whole bit—

LYNNE: I could actually see the back of their hooves through the windshield, we were that close.

JOHN: Miracle we didn't hit 'em... or wrap the Tesla around a goddamn tree.

EMILY: You're very lucky.

PAUL: Or a helluva driver.

LEWIS: Elk don't usually come down this far. Probably running from the fire.

JOHN: Lewis!

JOHN moves to put his phone in his pocket so he can shake LEWIS's hand.

NICOLE: Uh-uh, John. Time to surrender.

PAUL: Jesus, Nick. Lay off for a minute. Let the guy arrive.

JOHN: She's on it! I like it. You know, I paid some big shot executive coach to maximize my output—

LYNNE: To streamline. He was good.

JOHN: Five hundred bucks an hour for some guy to tell me to turn off my phone—and Nicole's figured it out with a basket!

JOHN drops his phone in the basket and hands NICOLE the wine.

I like the rules. And here's the wine, as promised. Don't put it in the fridge.

NICOLE: I wouldn't dream of it. Thank you, John.

JOHN: Added the free-weights, didn't you?

NICOLE: *(Flexing her arm.)* I did.

JOHN: And you, what are you lifting these days?

He slaps PAUL on the belly.

PAUL: Hey, this is all six-pack, my friend. Pure Pale Ale!

LYNNE drops her phone in the basket.

LYNNE: This retreat I just did in Bali, there was no technology at all—no cell phones, no WiFi.

EMILY: You guys went to Bali?

JOHN: Just Lynne. A thousand bucks a day for cold showers and a cot. Somebody enlighten me, please?

He kisses EMILY's cheek.

Emily, look at you! Did I hear you guys moved out to a place on the lake?

EMILY: Well, it's not right on the lake. Those places are all Airbnbs now. But it's close to the high school. Perfect for work.

LYNNE: I bet it's great. I can't believe we haven't seen it! So, where are the babies? I want my hugs!

EMILY: Our big baby is looking after their little babies at our place.

LYNNE: No! The kids aren't here?

NICOLE: Not tonight. Adults only. No kids, no phones and—

LYNNE: No business talk. I promise.

EMILY: And no politics.

JOHN: What's left?

LEWIS: Religion?

PAUL: Be a short conversation.

JOHN: How about sex? Can we talk about sex?

EMILY: A little bit of sex is okay.

JOHN: A little bit of sex is okay! Spoken like a woman who's been married for twenty-five years!

He walks over to LEWIS.

How are you, Lewis? You catch anything this summer?

LEWIS: Couple kokanee. I haven't been out on the lake much.

PAUL eats more cheese.

PAUL: No kidding, he even bailed on our annual fishing trip.

LEWIS: I didn't bail. I had a job.

PAUL: —Nearly 30 years of tradition blown off... for what? To make a few bucks—

JOHN ignores PAUL.

JOHN: You working a lot?

LEWIS: Much as I can.

NICOLE: Paul, come on, you should turn on the barbecue...

PAUL: Ready to go. Just say the word and—we will feast!

PAUL whips the cloth off the plate on the counter to reveal an impressive display of raw beef. They all gather around it.

EMILY: Oh my God.

JOHN: Will you look at that!

LEWIS whistles appreciatively.

PAUL: Highest grade, grass fed, organic beef.

LEWIS: Did you buy the whole cow?

EMILY: We are not going to eat all that.

PAUL: Just the best parts. You guys can take some for your freezer. If you don't mind pushing the rabbit and the frickin' gophers out of the way.

LEWIS: Fuck off.

JOHN: Where'd you get it?

PAUL: The meat? I got a guy.

JOHN: He's got a guy.

LYNNE: They always have a guy.

PAUL: Yeah, but my guy is the guy who gets it for all the other guys. He's THE guy.

EMILY: There's no room in our freezer, anyway.

PAUL: Make room. This is top quality beef. Alberta raised.

NICOLE: You filled that huge freezer in your garage?

JOHN: Hunting?

LEWIS: Costco.

EMILY: No, Lewis. It's the wolf.

NICOLE: The what?

They all look at LEWIS.

LEWIS: It's just the hide, Em.

EMILY: And the head. In the freezer. Don't forget her head.

LYNNE: Her?

JOHN: What?

LEWIS: She-wolf. A Grey.

JOHN: You shot a wolf?

LEWIS: No. I found her. I was hiking in the mountains north of here. Some of the old trappers are working with the government up there—

JOHN: You're talking about the wolf cull...

LEWIS: That's right. She'd got herself caught in a trap—

NICOLE: Oh, no.

LYNNE: Terrible.

JOHN: So, you brought the body home with you?

PAUL: You could probably get like, what, seventy-five bucks for the hide. Head's probably worth something, too.

LEWIS: Not to sell it.

PAUL: Then what?

LEWIS: I don't know. I couldn't just leave her there...

PAUL: Gonna be a pretty pissed-off trapper, finds out you stole his wolf.

JOHN: So you brought it home and...?

LEWIS: I never worked on a wolf before. It's different than a deer. Skin is thinner and more fragile, so it can spoil real fast. You have to get the pelt off before the slippage starts.

PAUL: Jesus.

JOHN: How did you know how to do that?

PAUL: He's the original mountain man.

LEWIS: I have a couple buddies who hunt.

JOHN: What the hell is "slippage"?

EMILY: Oh God. Don't ask.

LEWIS: Wolves hold a lot of heat in, even after they die. Thick fur, right? Keeps 'em warm. But the heat can create bacteria that gets into the skin, and if decomposition starts, you're finished. It causes the hair and bits of skin to loosen and come off, you can't get a clean cut on the hide... and she rots out completely. It's challenging.

EMILY: You should have seen the floor of the garage.

LEWIS: Yeah, well, she had a bellyful, so I had to hang her and—

PAUL slaps LEWIS on the back.

PAUL: Okay, I think we get the picture. C'mon, let's put this meat on and get the party started!

LEWIS: Sorry.

JOHN: Fascinating.

PAUL: John, grab your drink. Come see where we're going to put the pool.

PAUL winks at NICOLE. She shakes her head.

JOHN: Be right out.

LEWIS and PAUL exit. JOHN pauses to pull out a white envelope from his jacket pocket and sticks it into the flowers.

LYNNE: What's that?

JOHN: Just a card I picked up to go with the flowers. *(To EMILY.)* For later. Happy twenty-fifth anniversary.

EMILY: Thank you, John.

LYNNE gives him a look. JOHN exits.

Scene Two: Dining Room

Lights up mid-action at the dining table. NICOLE brings dishes to the table. EMILY and LYNNE help. JOHN uncorks the wine. PAUL holds up a giant piece of barbecued meat.

PAUL: Okay, Em, guest of honour first. Hand me your plate!

EMILY: Oh my God, that's huge.

PAUL: That's what all the ladies say.

EMILY: Give it to one of the guys.

PAUL: *(Under his breath.)* Never heard that before.

PAUL drops the meat back on the platter.

EMILY: The table looks so nice. These napkins are so pretty.

NICOLE: They're bamboo.

LYNNE points at the chandelier. EMILY clocks the conversation.

LYNNE: *(To NICOLE.)* I knew that chandelier would work perfectly over the table. When did you get it?

NICOLE: I ordered it right when we got back from Mexico.

LYNNE: Paul went for it?

NICOLE: I didn't ask him.

LYNNE: And that view. Amazing.

NICOLE: It's so much better without the smoke.

EMILY: Scary how the fires are every summer now.

LYNNE: The new normal.

NICOLE: I hope they get it contained soon. The smoke's really irritating Sierra's asthma. You packed her inhaler, the blue one, right, Paul?

PAUL: Yes. Sit, everyone!

NICOLE: Emily, you here, and Lewis here beside you. Come on. It's your night.

PAUL: Lynne, tenderloin, right?

LYNNE: I'm just going to do the veggies tonight.

PAUL: What?

NICOLE: You're not eating meat?

LYNNE: I've kind of gone off it.

Everyone stops and looks at the meat.

PAUL: Since when?

JOHN: Since her enlightenment.

LYNNE: That's not—

EMILY: So you're a vegetarian now?

LYNNE: It's just something I'm trying out.

PAUL: Well, you're missing out on some fine beef, woman.

NICOLE: We have lots of salad.

LYNNE: Perfect. Lewis, I die every time I see this table. I love it. Have you made any more?

LEWIS: I did a smaller one for Jacob's apartment.

LYNNE: *(To EMILY.)* How is my handsome godson doing?

EMILY: He's good. Really good.

LYNNE: We need to drop by the restaurant and say "Hi," John.

JOHN: Absolutely.

EMILY: He'd like that.

LEWIS: They keep him pretty busy.

PAUL: That kid sure makes a mean steak.

JOHN: So he's still excited about cooking?

EMILY: Loves it. Marcel has been such a mentor. And really... you know, understanding about Jacob taking time off when... I'm really grateful you introduced them.

JOHN: Glad to help. How old is he now? Well, he's got to be twenty-five, right?

EMILY: Right. Twenty-five.

JOHN: And he's still on the line? What about his aspirations to be a chef?

LEWIS: He is a chef.

EMILY: He's the sous chef now.

JOHN: But wasn't Europe in the plan... get some Michelin training under his belt?

NICOLE: He could get that in Vancouver now.

JOHN: Vancouver is not Europe.

EMILY: We like that he's in Vancouver, for now. Close. Enough. He may still go—

LYNNE: That kid could do anything he puts his mind to. And the great thing about cooking is you can always fall back on it.

EMILY: He likes to cook.

LYNNE: He's still young.

EMILY: Cooking is a profession.

LYNNE: He's so bright. He'll figure it out.

NICOLE puts her hand on EMILY's.

NICOLE: I'd want him close, too. If he were mine.

JOHN: Hard work, that's for sure.

NICOLE: Is he still in that cute little studio on Homer Street?

LEWIS: Yup. I think the table takes up half of it.

LYNNE: Seriously, Lewis. You could make a fortune selling these in New York.

EMILY: Lewis is putting together a website, with pictures for his woodworking business, right, honey?

LEWIS: Starting to...

EMILY: He's made a lot of beautiful pieces. He doesn't think of it as a money-making—

LEWIS: Em... PAUL: Emily, plate!

JOHN: You don't think this is worth something, Lewis?

LEWIS: It's not that. It just... It's not really about the money... it takes time... to do this right. *(Runs his hand on the table.)* Like the varnish...

LYNNE: How many coats?

LEWIS: Twenty-four.

JOHN: You're kidding.

LYNNE: We just saw the new Murakami exhibit. He does these amazing huge murals. Like a Japanese Andy Warhol. You know they all come from his head, but he's got teams working for him. Fulfilling his vision.

JOHN: Right. You could design 'em, cut the pieces. Get a team to do the assembly and varnish.

LEWIS: I guess I like seeing a piece through to the end.

JOHN: An artist. I respect that.

LEWIS: I don't know if I'm an artist—

LYNNE: Of course you are.

LEWIS: Well, I'm a guy who can't make a living making tables—

JOHN: So you're a true artist!

JOHN pours a glass of wine and sniffs it.

PAUL: Wait, did I just see— Hey Nick, did you see that?

NICOLE: I sure did.

JOHN: Hey, I'm just—

LYNNE: Don't look at me. You sniffed.

PAUL: Come on, tell us about the wine.

LEWIS: Enlighten us, man.

EMILY: We want to learn.

JOHN: All right. All right. This is a 1990 Centenaire from Les Cailloux. A special cuvée made largely from old Grenache vines with a touch of Syrah and Mourvedre.

LEWIS: A *touch* of Syrah.

EMILY: Shh.

JOHN swirls the wine, tilts the glass into the light.

JOHN: Dark raspberry colour, slight bricking towards the edges, good legs. *(Sniffs.)* Tart fruity nose... *(Tastes.)* A classic Grenache flavour... smooth, sweet, powerful. *(Swallows.)* With a long finish.

JOHN opens his eyes. The others burst out laughing.

To hell with you guys!

JOHN goes around the table pouring the wine.

You laugh, but each wine has a distinct personality. Each has its own story, its own provenance. Where the grapes are picked. When they're picked. The light. The soil. That's the DNA. But the care... the care that's given— A good wine is nurtured. Like... like a...

NICOLE: ... like a child?

JOHN pauses at NICOLE's remark.

JOHN: ...like a child.

EMILY sips, swirls the wine in her mouth.

EMILY: That's so lovely. I can taste the—

PAUL: Syrah?

EMILY: No, Paul. The complexity. It's delicious.

JOHN: I'm pleased you like it.

LEWIS: I think I had more of a six-pack "provenance."

PAUL: Totally. *(Then to JOHN.)* Striploin, right?

JOHN: Lean and mean.

PAUL: Lewis, plate! Look at this baby. Best cut for my best friend. Bone-in rib eye.

LEWIS passes his plate forward. PAUL holds up a huge piece of steak and dumps it on LEWIS's plate.

EMILY: Are you really going to eat all that?

PAUL: You're asking the only guy who ever finished the entire Grizzly if he's gonna eat all that?

JOHN: The what?

PAUL: The Grizzly. This humongous breakfast at—

LYNNE: The Trapper!

EMILY: The *Lonely* Trapper.

NICOLE: Why was he lonely?

LEWIS: Probably because he was such a crappy cook.

PAUL: Come on, best greasy breakfast in town.

JOHN: And the Grizzly was...?

PAUL/LEWIS: Four eggs, four pieces of toast, four slices of bacon, four sausages... Four pancakes and four waffles, and... trapper fries!

NICOLE: You ate all that?

LEWIS: I had to. Paul bet me five bucks that I couldn't.

NICOLE: Of course he did.

JOHN: And it was free if you ate the whole thing, right?

LEWIS: No way. All you got was this cheap little plastic grizzly doll on a keychain.

LYNNE: *(Thoughtful.)* That's right.

EMILY: *(Jumping in.)* We were all so wasted that night. It was gross.

JOHN: That night?

LYNNE shoots EMILY a look. LEWIS picks up on it.

LEWIS: I was sober enough to remember you still owe me five bucks, buddy.

NICOLE: Of course he does.

JOHN: *(To LYNNE.)* I thought you weren't allowed to drink.

LYNNE: I wasn't "allowed." We had to sneak out into the Orchard. You know how strict my parents were.

EMILY: Your mom was sweet.

PAUL: Best sour cherry pie on the planet—

LYNNE: "You too skinny, Paul!"

NICOLE: Skinny?

LYNNE: What *was* that stuff we drank out there?

EMILY/
LEWIS: Lucky Lager!

PAUL: "Borrowed" from my dad's garage.

LEWIS: Sure smelled nice, all those fruit trees.

EMILY: And the stars—

LYNNE: Were amazing back then.

LEWIS: No lights from the city.

EMILY: *(Aside to LEWIS.)* ...that itchy grass—

PAUL: Lewis on guitar.

EMILY: Oh my God, "Stairway to Heaven." Over and over—

PAUL: And over. Did you ever learn another song—

LEWIS: What for?

The four laugh.

LYNNE: It's still my favourite place in the world.

NICOLE: I can see why you'd want to hold onto it.

EMILY: I thought you were selling it?

LYNNE: I was going to... After I moved my parents down to the city, we had three offers to develop the property for condos—

JOHN: Everybody wants their little piece of what you have here.

EMILY: God, I wish we'd bought our piece.

LEWIS: Em...

LYNNE: I just couldn't bear the thought of bulldozing those beautiful orchards my family had worked on for generations. So when Paul suggested we develop it ourselves—

JOHN: Paul actually suggested condos—

PAUL: Not exactly—

LYNNE: Anyway, it made me think about how I could do something different with it—even if the fruit business isn't viable anymore, there are ways to develop and keep some of the land intact.

JOHN: Eco-tourism.

PAUL: Pays for itself.

JOHN: A win-win.

LYNNE: I want to keep a few of the groves, so people can enjoy them the way we used to—it could be really special. Show people what we have here.

EMILY: We get a lot of tourists, people seem to know what's here—

LYNNE: This is going to be a whole other level.

JOHN: *(To PAUL.)* Where are we with the permits?

PAUL: I'm on it. It's a little tricky these days.

LEWIS: Sounds like you guys are going into business together.

JOHN: We're still working out the details.

EMILY: Wow, when did this all happen?

LYNNE: When we were down in Mexico. You know, I've designed much bigger projects, but I feel like this is the most important one I've ever worked on in my life.

JOHN: Because it's personal.

LYNNE: It is. It really is.

LYNNE reaches out and takes JOHN's hand.

EMILY: Exciting.

LYNNE: Oh God, I'm sorry, Nicole, I guess this is venturing into business territory, isn't it?

A cellphone rings in the basket. They all look at NICOLE.

JOHN: Someone's in trouble.

PAUL: *(To NICOLE.)* That's you.

JOHN: I see. Rules are made to be broken... as long as you make them, right?

NICOLE: No. I just have to leave it on for the kids—

PAUL: But if that was my phone going off— *(Mouths the word.)* C a s t r a t i o n.

NICOLE: Stop. I'll only answer if it's the girls... See, it's Sierra. *(Into the phone.)* Hi, honey. *(To the room.)* We have to have one phone on, if something happens— *(Into the phone.)* What do you need, sweetie?

EMILY: Maybe it's her asthma?

LEWIS: Annie knows how to look after her.

NICOLE: *(Into phone.)* Don't cry—

PAUL:	Is she all right?	LYNNE:	I hope she's okay.

NICOLE: *(Into phone.)* Okay. Don't get upset. Just take a deep breath. *(Pause.)* You have my credit card on your phone, right? *(To PAUL.)* They want to order Dine and Deliver from Nobi's...

EMILY: What? We left them a lasagna for dinner.

NICOLE: She's not doing carbs, I forgot to tell you.

EMILY:	There's a Caesar salad there, too.	LEWIS:	The fridge is full of—

JOHN: Looks like we have our emergency. CARBS.

PAUL: Just tell her to use the card.

NICOLE: Daddy says use the card, just get Annie to give them the address. Of course, order for everyone. Remember no wasabi for Sam on his California roll. Okay. Love you, too.

EMILY: There's a whole dinner there in the fridge. You don't have to order for Annie—

NICOLE: Special treat. It's on us. Anything to keep the peace tonight.

EMILY: I didn't know about the carbs thing. I could've made chicken.

LYNNE: She's nine. Is she watching her weight?

NICOLE: It's just something she's trying out.

LYNNE: Body dysmorphia starts really young. The way young girls are taught to see themselves—

NICOLE: She doesn't have body dysmorphia.

EMILY: Of course not—

LYNNE: I understand—she wants to be fit like her mom.

JOHN: Good thing you had your phone on. Lasagna avoided. Emergency handled, right?

PAUL: Right.

NICOLE: Okay, enough about my phone. See, it's in the basket. All right, everybody, I have a game!

PAUL: Oh God. LYNNE: Uh oh.

JOHN: Here we go... EMILY: I want to hear!

PAUL: Honey. We love you. But your games aren't fun.

NICOLE: What, my games are fun! I'm fun. Right, guys?

PAUL: You're fun. Your games—

NICOLE: Lewis?

LEWIS: This asparagus is delicious.

NICOLE: C'mon, it's just a little one. About marriage... for your anniversary. One word each. Please?

EMILY: I want to play.

NICOLE passes around index cards and pencils.

NICOLE: There you go. It's Emily's party. Okay. This is what we do. I can feel you rolling your eyes, Paul, stop. All we do is write down the word that you believe is the most important quality of a successful marriage, then we share—

PAUL: Do we have to write it down? I hate games where you have to write. It's like school.

NICOLE: Paul! It's just one word.

JOHN: Do we get points? Like for the best word?

PAUL: Or prizes?

NICOLE: You get to sleep in the house tonight.

PAUL: Okay, okay. I'll start. LOVE. Marriage is love.

NICOLE: You didn't even think about it.

PAUL: I don't need to think. Love is obvious, right. Marriage is love. What, you get to critique my word?

EMILY: "Love" is good. I think I would have said "love."

NICOLE: Okay. Write it down, Paul. Lynne?

LYNNE: I think "respect." No, wait, "understanding." You have to really try to understand your partner. I don't think you can have a marriage without understanding.

NICOLE: Good one.

JOHN: Or trust.

NICOLE: Is that yours?

JOHN: Absolutely. You can't have a marriage without trust. When that goes, the boat sinks.

NICOLE: See, these are good. Love, Understanding, Trust. I'll say, "respect." Respect is vital. Em?

EMILY: Umm. Hmmm... well, passion is important, right? Keeping the fires burning.... and companionship... friendship... and I like understanding... because you have to understand what the other person needs and wants... respect, too...

PAUL: Jesus. Is there a single word in there?

EMILY: Okay, okay, do I just get one? Right. I'd say... well, I guess, "love." It has to be "love."

PAUL: Is she allowed to say mine? That's my word.

NICOLE: She can have "love," it's her party. You think of another one.

PAUL crosses out his word and writes another one.

PAUL: Okay. How about "sex"? Gotta have sex.

NICOLE: Fine. Lewis?

LEWIS answers without looking up from his plate.

LEWIS: Compromise. Marriage is compromise.

EMILY: What? That's your word. "Compromise"?

LYNNE: Oops.

LEWIS: Isn't that okay?

JOHN: It's definitely pragmatic.

EMILY: It's not very romantic.

JOHN: Marriage is not romantic.

EMILY / NICOLE / LYNNE What?!

PAUL: Here we go.

JOHN: I mean, technically, it's a contract.

NICOLE: Really?

LYNNE: It's more than that.

PAUL: Fun game.

LEWIS: Marriage is a lot of things. Nicole said, "Pick one word."

EMILY: And you picked "compromise." You didn't even think about it—

LEWIS: I was last. I thought about it while I was eating.

NICOLE picks up the little bonsai tree on the counter.

NICOLE: Okay wait, hold on. Now we do part two of the game—

PAUL: What? No.

JOHN: Uh oh. LYNNE: There's a part two?

NICOLE: Guys! See how you all have a little rock by your plate? All you have to do is paint your word on your rock tonight. Then, we put them under this little bonsai tree. And Emily and Lewis get to have it as a keepsake for their anniversary.

EMILY: I love it!

PAUL: This isn't a game, it's an art project.

NICOLE: It's one word on a rock, Paul. *(To the others.)* You can do it whenever you want. I've got paints and brushes right over here.

PAUL: And there's no part three, right?

NICOLE: Promise.

EMILY: This is so fun!

JOHN raises his glass. EMILY drains hers.

JOHN: Well, painting a rock definitely spans the breadth of my artistic ability, but I'm up for the challenge.

PAUL: Yes, John, that's what we need. A toast! To Emily and Lewis.

JOHN: *(Ignoring PAUL.)* So, Lewis, tell me, you for or against the wolf cull?

EMILY: Against it.

LEWIS: There's pros and cons. Guess it depends on how you look at it.

JOHN: And how *do* you look at it? I mean, there's been a lot of controversy. I figure you must have an inside track.

LEWIS: Why's that?

JOHN: You live here, you're out in the woods all the time. You fish, you hunt with your buddies. I just figured you guys must have a point of view. What, you're not interested?

LEWIS: I'm interested in wolves. Politics not so much.

JOHN: You think the cull is political?

LEWIS: Wolves have gotta eat, too.

LEWIS gets up and heads to the kitchen.

PAUL: Hey guys, you gonna let me make this toast or not? Lewis, where you going?

LEWIS: Perrier?

NICOLE: It's in there on the bottom shelf.

PAUL: Right next to the wolf head.

LEWIS: Ha, ha.

JOHN: So you agree that we're demonizing a group of highly intelligent animals who are just following a basic instinct, which is to feed off a weaker species.

NICOLE: But the caribou are endangered, right? We need to protect them.

EMILY: It's really about the logging and mining companies wanting the government to protect their rights... even though they're the ones destroying the caribou habitat. So they blame the wolves instead—

JOHN: Easy target. Big bad wolves— *(To LEWIS as he comes back.)* So, you do think the wolf cull is a smokescreen to protect special interest groups?

EMILY: Yes!

LEWIS: It's complicated. *(To JOHN.)* You sure you got that cut into small enough pieces?

JOHN: Old boarding school habit.

LYNNE: They did not teach you that at boarding school.

JOHN: *(Sharply.)* Did you go to boarding school?

LEWIS sets the Perrier bottle down by EMILY. Sits. EMILY ignores the Perrier and drinks her wine.

NICOLE: It just feels wrong to me. I mean, they're beautiful creatures, right?

LEWIS: They are.

EMILY: They're highly social. And they're loyal. They're like people that way.

JOHN: Some people.

NICOLE: I read somewhere they mate for life.

JOHN: Unlike most people.

LEWIS: People are emotional. Wolves aren't.

PAUL: So, my guess is wolves don't play the marriage game.

LYNNE: But shooting them out of a helicopter—

EMILY: Or trapping them. It's horrible.

PAUL: It's selective. Man trying to restore nature's balance.

LYNNE: Oh, and "MAN" is definitely right for the job. Look at Man's track record.

NICOLE: How do they decide which wolves to shoot? What if they cull the parents, what happens to the cubs? Are they called cubs?

LEWIS: Pups.

JOHN: They don't just shoot them randomly— Do they, Lewis?

NICOLE: What do you mean?

LEWIS pushes his plate away.

LEWIS: No. It's not random.

NICOLE: Meaning what?

Pause.

LEWIS: They take the whole pack.

PAUL: Jesus. LYNNE: What?

NICOLE: They shoot the babies?

LYNNE: No, they don't!

LEWIS: Only if they're old enough to hunt with the pack.

EMILY: And what happens to them if—

LEWIS: Wolves function as a unit. A family. They survive together. Or they don't survive at all.

EMILY: Like us.

JOHN: I think the idea is it's kinder to destroy the whole lot.

LYNNE: God, John.

JOHN: I don't support it. But I understand the logic.

NICOLE: I don't see why they have to shoot them at all. There must be another way—

LEWIS: There's always another way.

LYNNE: Well, I think we should let Nature take her course.

PAUL stands.

PAUL: Enough! Can we have our toast now?!

LYNNE: Right, a toast to Emily and Lewis.

PAUL: Now, if I can get serious for a moment... Don't worry, I promise to keep it short. I thought of all the things I could say about Em and Lewis tonight. Some crazy stories I could tell—

EMILY: Please don't. LYNNE: Uh-oh.

PAUL: But I kept coming back to this one day our senior year in high school... *(To LEWIS.)* ...you remember the day... when you came to tell me Em was pregnant. Said it just like that. "Em's pregnant." Man, I didn't have a clue what to say. And I start goin' on about how you didn't have to go through with it, how you could, you know... give up the baby, whatever. And the whole time you're just sitting there. Not saying a word. And when I'm finally done, you look at me, and you *grin*. That fucking grin. Classic Lewis. No money, no job... eighteen years old... and that's when I knew you guys were gonna have a baby! I figured you were both crazy, and it *was* crazy. Getting married. Lewis working two jobs, Em, a mom at seventeen changing diapers, and I saw how tough it was... the sacrifices you had to make. But I also got to see how that baby lit up your lives... Jacob... then Annie... and what terrific parents you became... through all the ups and downs... You guys did it right. Really. You're two of the finest people I know. And I feel, we all feel, honoured to be here with you celebrating your twenty-five years. To Em and Lewis!

NICOLE: To Em and Lewis!

LYNNE: We love you guys. JOHN: Nice.

EMILY: So nice.

LYNNE: Em, not allowed to cry.

EMILY: I'm not crying. Really. I'm just so grateful. For all of you. Seriously, sometimes it feels like... people out there... life just gets... but here with you guys... I needed this tonight.

NICOLE: Of course you do. You have so much on your plate. The kids, work, night school...

LEWIS: She's almost done. What... four more credits? *(EMILY nods.)* And she'll have her teaching degree.

LYNNE: That's fantastic. You are going to be such a wonderful teacher.

EMILY: It's not just me. Lewis hardly gets a weekend off anymore.

PAUL: Still, no excuse to bail on our fishing trip.

EMILY: Jacob really needs to see his counsellor once a week. He's so good. But it's expensive—

LEWIS: He's going to keep seeing his counsellor.

JOHN gestures to the card he's put on the table.

JOHN: Why don't you open your card, Emily?

EMILY: And the rents in Vancouver keep going up... if he can't afford the rent on his own... he's not good with roommates, you know.

She takes out the card, reads it.

LEWIS: We'll cross that bridge when we get there.

EMILY: Oh, that's lovely, you two. Thank you.

JOHN: I think there's something else in there.

EMILY shakes out the envelope, and a cheque falls onto the table. LYNNE gives JOHN a look.

EMILY: John?

JOHN: Maybe it'll help. With the counsellor. The rent. Whatever you like.

EMILY: Oh my God. What? Really?

LEWIS takes the cheque out of her hand and frowns.

PAUL: What is it?

LEWIS hands the cheque to PAUL who hands it to NICOLE.

PAUL: Holy shit.

LEWIS: We can't accept it.

EMILY: What—

NICOLE: Wow. I thought we said no gifts.

JOHN: Look, it's no big deal.

LEWIS: Twenty-five thousand dollars is kind of a big deal.

EMILY: It's very generous.

JOHN: Well, twenty-five years. It felt appropriate somehow.

LEWIS: We appreciate the gesture, John, really, but we can't—

JOHN: Why not? Come on, look, all of your kids are already in our legacy planning. Think of it as an early installment.

LEWIS: *(To LYNNE.)* Did you know about this?

LYNNE: *(Covering.)* Sure... of course. We want you to have it.

PAUL: Keep the wolf from the door.

LEWIS: The wolf is not at the door.

PAUL: Come on, it's not that big a deal, right? It's just money. Hell, we paid close to that for this thing—

PAUL points to the chandelier. EMILY glances at NICOLE.

NICOLE: We did not! Not anywhere near that much—

PAUL: Whatever. My point is, if the money can help, it's better spent on friends.

NICOLE: Of course. You two deserve it. And Lewis, your wife deserves a vacation.

LEWIS: I know she does.

EMILY: And so do you.

LEWIS: We'll figure it out. Sorry, John.

He hands the cheque back.

JOHN: Compromise. Right, Lewis?

LEWIS: This isn't about—

PAUL: Pride?

LEWIS: No.

An uncomfortable silence.

JOHN: Look, I didn't mean to—

EMILY: It's very generous, John. And thoughtful. But Lewis is right, we can't. It would be—

LEWIS: Wrong.

LYNNE: We understand. Right, John?

JOHN: Of course.

EMILY: Just being with you all is enough. I mean, look at this beautiful meal. The party. And my goodness, this is so delicious. The asparagus is so... organic, right? I mean that's so much better, isn't it? And the meat. Didn't you say it was grass-fed?

EMILY bursts into tears.

LYNNE: Emily?

EMILY: I'm sorry—

JOHN: I hope I didn't—

EMILY: *(In a rush of emotion.)* No, no, it's not you, it's not the cheque... It's just... it's just... I always try to buy the right thing, too... Like free range eggs... even though they're twice as expensive. Because I hate the idea of those poor chickens being all cooped up like that. It's not right. One on top of the other. I mean, it's better for them to run free, isn't it?

Puzzled looks from everyone.

LYNNE: Sure.

NICOLE: Right.

PAUL: We're talking about eggs?

EMILY: Then I find out "free range" means they only have to let the chickens out for an hour. One hour! And they just do it so they can print it on the package, so that people think they're—

JOHN: It's marketing.

EMILY: — they don't care about the chickens at all. It's like the chickens are kept in solitary confinement, and then they get their one hour out in the yard.

PAUL: Well, it's more like they're in an overcrowded prison, and they get their one hour—

NICOLE: Paul!

EMILY: I try to do the right thing. But I can't. At the supermarket. At the bank—

JOHN: What happened at the bank?

EMILY: It's like everywhere you go, they're lying to you. They send you all these credit card offers, but if you want a loan, they tell you you don't qualify. They have no problem charging 20% interest on your Visa balance, but you can't even cash in your mutual funds without—

JOHN: You don't want to cash in your—

EMILY: —paying a penalty. They make you pay a penalty! And then they only pay 2%! After all those hidden fees. 2%!

LEWIS: Em.

PAUL: You guys need a loan?

LEWIS: No.

EMILY: I'm sorry. But sometimes the whole thing makes me feel like one of those stupid chickens.

LYNNE: You're not a stupid chicken, Em.

LEWIS: Chickens aren't really that stupid. They've done studies. They're social. They're empathetic. They protect their young.

They all look at LEWIS, laugh. EMILY smiles.

PAUL: Are you kidding me—how do you know this stuff?

JOHN: Come talk to me about investing.

LEWIS: I don't think we're in your league, John.

JOHN: You're my friends. I'm serious. I can help you.

LEWIS: We'll work it out. *(Nudges EMILY.)* We'll put a chicken coop in the backyard.

EMILY I don't want chickens in my backyard.

LEWIS: Pigs?

EMILY blows her nose in the bamboo napkin.

EMILY: Stop! It's okay. Maybe I needed a good cry. I just hate that they lie to you.

JOHN: "They"?

EMILY: The banks, the politicians, the—

PAUL: —chicken farmers?

EMILY: They lead you to assume things are a certain way, when really... they're not.

JOHN: Well, that's kind of the way things work, isn't it? If you want to feel good about eating "free range" chicken twice a week, maybe you have to swallow a few—

NICOLE: Lies?

JOHN: Did you ever consider that it's part of the deal we make?

NICOLE: What's that supposed to mean?

JOHN: Simple, Nicole. It means that we go along with the "lies" as long as it's in our self-interest to believe them. It's only when they stop working for us that we get upset.

NICOLE: Not everything is a deal, John.

EMILY: I just want to do the right thing.

NICOLE: Of course you do. We all do. It's human nature.

JOHN: Is it? And what does that even mean, "doing the right thing"?

NICOLE: Come on, John. Being responsible. Buying locally sourced food, recycling, protecting the environment...

JOHN: Right. So we can all feel better about having more stuff.

NICOLE: What?!

JOHN raises his bamboo napkin.

JOHN: Look, bamboo napkins are a nice idea, but come on.

LYNNE: Don't be so cynical, John. Off-gassing from cheap synthetics is toxic, you know that. *(Folds her napkin.)* Bamboo napkins are a good place to start.

EMILY: And they're very pretty.

NICOLE: Some of us just want to do our part.

JOHN: That's great. I just think the whole sustainable living thing has become a bit of a charade—a game we play for each other. Rolling up our plastic and sending it off to Bangladesh, hundred-thousand-dollar electric cars— Isn't it all just a way to have everything we want without making any real sacrifice?

LEWIS: What about having less stuff?

JOHN: There's a plan. How about having less stuff, Nicole?

NICOLE: I agree.

PAUL: Really?

NICOLE: *(To PAUL.)* It's a good place to start. *(To JOHN.)* You drive a Tesla, John!

JOHN: Not because I think it'll save the world. It's a beautiful idea. One that probably came too late.

LEWIS: Too late?

NICOLE: People are marching in the streets to try and change things—

JOHN: Yeah. And I'm saying I don't think we're capable of change. If we really cared, we'd never get on an airplane again. But who is willing to do that? Hell, there are six people at this table, and five of us aren't even willing to give up meat.

PAUL: Personally, I'd rather give up flying.

LYNNE: Methane gas does just as much damage.

JOHN: The whole human experiment may be doomed in the first place. Certainly if we're waiting around for people to "do the right thing."

NICOLE: It still matters what we do. We always have a choice.

JOHN: Or we like to think we do. I believe we're living out the consequences for choices we made a long time ago. It's a done deal.

LEWIS: So just exploit it—ride it 'til the end?

LYNNE: You don't believe that, John. You're just being contrary. Climate change is the defining issue of our time. We're all catching up to the truth. When we know better, we do better.

JOHN: No, we don't. It really depends on what we value. People don't like to change. We do as little as possible to stay as comfortable as possible.

NICOLE: Well, I value my children.

JOHN: I'm sure you do.

NICOLE: Maybe you have to be a parent to understand that it's possible to care about the next generation.

PAUL: Jesus, Nicole—

LYNNE: That's not what she meant—

JOHN: I'm not talking about the next generation, I'm talking about how we behave now.

LEWIS: I'm thinking this is not something we can resolve at a dinner party.

JOHN: Changing for the good is hard and slow. Time may have the upper hand here. I'm sorry if that upsets you.

NICOLE: So don't even try?

PAUL: Time to put this in the basket, guys.

JOHN: Look, we do what we can. We help who we can. We enjoy what we can. So sure, try. Just don't lie to yourself.

NICOLE: Oh, I'm lying to myself because I want to make a difference? Some of us have values.

JOHN:	We all have values. I'm just curious how your values differ from mine? You like nice things. I like nice things. I just don't tell myself a big story about it.
NICOLE:	We are not the same.
LYNNE:	John—
JOHN:	You can't have it both ways, Nicole. You can't build a twelve-thousand-square-foot house and honestly say that having less stuff is "a good place to start."
NICOLE:	I was agreeing with Lewis that—
JOHN:	C'mon, you're either on the boat or you're off the boat.
NICOLE:	Right! And just kick people off the boat if they get in your way?
JOHN:	What?
NICOLE:	What gives *you* the right to jump the line?
PAUL:	Nicole—
JOHN:	Are you talking about Mexico?
NICOLE:	You kicked those people off the boat —
JOHN:	I paid them.
NICOLE:	You paid the driver.
JOHN:	We made a deal. And you agreed to that deal when you and *your children* "jumped the line" to get on that boat. Maybe what's really bothering you is all those people who saw you do it. But you know what, you still got on the boat. Didn't you?
NICOLE:	I had to!

JOHN: Really? I thought you "always had a choice"?

NICOLE falters.

PAUL: The Mexicans were fine with it.

JOHN: They didn't have a choice. They needed the money.

NICOLE: God, I cannot believe this—

JOHN: Like it or not, Nicole, it's the way things work. The sad truth is, most people in the world are like those chickens. And we're the wolves.

PAUL: Wolves in the henhouse.

NICOLE: Fox! It's fox in the henhouse.

PAUL: Fox, wolf. Same difference.

LEWIS: Not really.

LYNNE: So, you're either a wolf or a chicken? That sounds pretty simplistic.

LEWIS: And self-serving.

PAUL: I want to be a wolf. Alpha, here!

NICOLE: Why do you get to be the Alpha?

PAUL: I brought the meat! Right, Lewis?

LEWIS: Whatever you say.

NICOLE: I'm pretty sure John thinks he's the Alpha.

EMILY: Why does the Alpha have to be a male?

LEWIS: Actually, it's usually an Alpha couple. A male and a female.

LYNNE: That's more like it.

JOHN: And what makes them the Alpha couple?

NICOLE: Not their hedge fund, John.

JOHN: You sure about that, Nicole?

PAUL: They're the strongest.

LEWIS nods.

LEWIS: The Alphas are the only ones who mate and have pups.

JOHN: Well, there it is. Can't have kids. Can't be head of the pack. *(To LYNNE.)* Guess we're outta luck, babe.

LYNNE: We're not wolves.

LEWIS: No, we're sure as hell not.

JOHN: But we are predators.

LEWIS: Except wolves are driven by the needs of the pack, the greater good. It's in their DNA, it's how they survive as a species.

JOHN: Whereas people are driven by self-interest. My point exactly.

EMILY: Not all people.

NICOLE: Of course not.

JOHN: Show me someone who isn't.

EMILY: We're all friends. We care about each other. Look how generous you've been tonight.

JOHN: I can afford to be generous. It's a luxury of having money. Everyone wants to look after their friends and family...if they can.

EMILY: I still don't believe you're all about self-interest, John.

NICOLE: Hah. LYNNE: Of course he's not.

JOHN: Why is self-interest so bad, or surprising for that matter? Protecting your interests is human nature. And it's the nature of business.

JOHN takes the cheque out of his pocket and writes on it.

JOHN: I should have known you'd never accept this. I've got a better idea. One that works for my self-interest and yours. Why don't we consider this a job offer?

He hands the cheque to LEWIS.

LEWIS: What is this?

JOHN: A year's salary... in advance. To come work on the Orchard project with us.

PAUL and LYNNE exchange a glance. A total surprise.

LEWIS: Two-hundred-and-fifty-thousand dollars?

EMILY: What?!

LEWIS hands EMILY the cheque.

JOHN: You'll earn it.

PAUL: That's a helluva lot of cabinets.

JOHN: Not just cabinets.

LEWIS: What else?

JOHN: You'll design *all* the furniture, all the finishings... everything custom, completely original. We want to attract people willing to spend some real money for an authentic experience... If they like the hand-carved dining table in their unit, they can buy it. You won't even need a website.

LYNNE: John—

JOHN: This is a chance to do what you love. Make something beautiful. And get paid for it. All the furnishings for the lodge and thirty self-contained units.

LEWIS: Thirty units. How would I—

JOHN: You'd hire a team. Oversee everything. Build it all in your own workshop on site. You could even offer woodworking seminars—

LYNNE: John—

JOHN: *(To LYNNE.)* —as part of the experience. Sandpaper and turn down service. People *care* about how things are made. *(To LEWIS.)* Like you care, Lewis. And what's more—

LYNNE: Would you please STOP!

JOHN: Excuse me?

LYNNE: You're doing it. Again. Taking control.

JOHN: Uh-oh, here we go—

LYNNE: We're a team.

JOHN: Exactly. And you're going to lead the team.

LYNNE: Yes. Like we agreed. This was my idea. My vision. My land.

JOHN: And my money—

LYNNE: And Paul's.

JOHN: So this is about Paul?

PAUL: What?

LYNNE: Of course not. It's about all of us. We're all invested, John. We're partners. Right?

A moment.

JOHN: Okay, okay, I got carried away. I'm an asshole. But c'mon, hiring Lewis is a great idea, right?

LYNNE: It's a brilliant idea. I should have thought of it myself. What about it, Lewis?

LEWIS: You're serious.

LYNNE: Completely. I can't think of a better person for the job.

LEWIS: *(To PAUL.)* What do you think, buddy?

PAUL: Fantastic. I mean, we need to iron out a few details.

NICOLE: Exciting. All of you working together.

LYNNE: It's perfect.

LEWIS hesitates. JOHN pushes away from the table.

JOHN: You know what, I'd like to see that new humidor, Paul!

PAUL: There's an idea. How about a nice Cuban cigar. Lewis?

LEWIS looks to EMILY.

EMILY: It's an amazing opportunity...

Pause.

LEWIS: Yeah, I could smoke a cigar.

JOHN: That's what I'm talking about! *(Hands up, correcting himself.) We're* talking about!

Laughter. EMILY helps NICOLE clear dishes as the others start to leave.

NICOLE: It's okay, guys, don't worry, we've got this.

LEWIS turns back.

Kidding, Lewis! Go smoke your cigar.

LYNNE stops JOHN.

LYNNE: John?

JOHN: *(To the guys.)* I'll be right there.

LYNNE waits until they are alone.

LYNNE: Are we good?

JOHN: Sure.

LYNNE: You promised me...

JOHN: We're good. At least, I'm good. I'm sorry, do you want to go smoke the cigar?

LYNNE: Go smoke your cigar.

JOHN kisses her. Exits.

LYNNE waits, checks to make sure she is alone. Then picks up a piece of steak off the platter and rips at it with her teeth, hungrily. Lights to black.

Scene Three: Den

The flare of PAUL lighting his cigar brings the lights up. PAUL paces. LEWIS sits.

PAUL: Weird, huh?

LEWIS: You okay with this?

PAUL: Sure. Of course. I don't think he had to be so fucking dramatic about it... but yeah, it's a great idea. Good money, great job.

LEWIS: I don't know. Feels kinda funny.

PAUL: You think too much, Lewis.

LEWIS: Are you pissed at me?

PAUL: What? No. I'm happy for you. About time you guys caught a break. At least this way, you won't have an excuse to bail on our fishing trip next year.

LEWIS: Hey, I take this job, who's gonna have time for fishing?

PAUL: Bullshit. Priorities... Job or no job, we make the time. Okay?

LEWIS: Deal.

JOHN enters and takes the chair next to LEWIS.

PAUL: —Hey, there he is! How about a Cohiba?

JOHN: Nice. *(To LEWIS.)* You make the humidor?

LEWIS: Nope. Not my thing.

PAUL: I got this guy in Vancouver—

JOHN: *(To LEWIS.)* —I didn't mean to put you on the spot out there, but I figured, hell, what better time than your twenty-fifth anniversary?

LEWIS: Hell of a surprise.

JOHN: Salary's totally negotiable. Just kind of fun adding that extra zero. I like things to line up.

LEWIS: It's very generous.

JOHN: You gonna stand there and hover, Paul?

PAUL: Huh?

JOHN: Why don't you sit?

PAUL sits. JOHN lights his cigar.

JOHN: You did yourself proud with those steaks.

PAUL: Thanks.

JOHN: So. How's Artie?

PAUL: Artie? He's good.

JOHN: *(To LEWIS.)* Big investor in the project. One of Paul's "guys."

PAUL: We're sorting it out.

LEWIS: *(To PAUL.)* You want me to leave?

JOHN: No, you're part of this now. No secrets here. Right, Paul?

PAUL: Nope. It's all covered. So, how about a brandy to celebrate Lewis taking the job?

LEWIS: I still need to think about the job, you guys.

PAUL: Jesus Christ, Lewis!

JOHN: I get it. Talk it over with Em, let us know. Of course, this isn't just about the money, right? It's about all of us working together. It means a lot to Lynne.

PAUL: That's the beauty of it. Friends working together.

JOHN: Exactly. We just gotta find a way to keep you in.

PAUL: I am in.

JOHN: As long as you come up with your 25%.

PAUL: I already have—

JOHN: Half.

PAUL: I'm just waiting on Artie.

JOHN: Right. You're sorting it out. You said that.

PAUL: Hey, I'm a respected contractor in this town. He'll come through.

Beat.

JOHN laughs. Slaps PAUL on the back.

JOHN: Relax, man. I'm just fucking with you. Let's have that drink!

LEWIS meets PAUL's eyes.

Scene Four: Kitchen

In the kitchen, EMILY and NICOLE tidy up.

EMILY: ...and with Lewis working a regular schedule, I could take a few extra trips to the city. See Jacob more. Maybe even take that vacation...

NICOLE: *(Distracted.)* Funny how things work out...

LYNNE enters.

Everything all right?

LYNNE: Fine. Look, I'm sorry about all that earlier... with John.

NICOLE: You don't have to apologize for him.

LYNNE: He can be pretty damn opinionated.

NICOLE: No kidding.

LYNNE: Well, he's always been confident. It's part of his charm.

NICOLE: He's definitely sure of himself.

LYNNE: Yeah, I guess he's not as easygoing as some men.

NICOLE: You mean Paul?

EMILY bumps into NICOLE as she moves a plate.

(Sharply.) Emily, stop! You don't need to help here.

EMILY: Excuse me?

NICOLE: I'm sorry, I just mean, you shouldn't be doing the dishes, right? It's your party.

EMILY: Right.

LYNNE: It's a big night. Lots to celebrate.

NICOLE: Exactly. Why don't you take your wine to the terrace and let Lynne and me finish up? Don't want to spoil any *surprises*, right?

EMILY: Oh, right. Of course not. I'll just go out to the terrace.

EMILY exits to the terrace with her wine.

NICOLE takes a large cake out of its box.

LYNNE: Wow!

NICOLE: Paul ordered it.

LYNNE: Of course he did. Think it's big enough? What a nut. Like the way he orders at a restaurant, right?

NICOLE: Practically everything on the menu.

LYNNE: It's fun.

NICOLE: Is it?

LYNNE: His enthusiasm for food, for life. He's always been like that. He wants to taste it all.

NICOLE: He certainly does.

LYNNE: Like a big kid.

NICOLE: Did you and John ever talk about adopting again? I mean, you mentioned it in Mexico...

LYNNE hesitates.

LYNNE: That conversation is over. If it's not his DNA, he isn't interested.

NICOLE: I'm sorry. That can't be easy for you.

LYNNE: You know what, I realize I've made peace with it. Maybe that's what I connected with in Bali. That inner voice. You need to get really quiet to hear it.

NICOLE: Right. Well, I guess it's easier to get quiet when you don't have a couple kids running around.

LYNNE: *(Tightly.)* Right.

NICOLE: Okay then. All we need is candles.

Scene Five: Terrace

On the terrace, EMILY with her wine; LEWIS stares out at the distant glow in the sky.

LEWIS: Wind's changing. Bringing the fire closer down the mountain...

EMILY: Lewis?

LEWIS: All those trees.

EMILY: Paul said it's going to rain. That'll help.

LEWIS: Maybe.

EMILY: Are you going to tell me what you said to John?

LEWIS: I said I'd think about it.

Pause.

EMILY: Think about it, like you'll think about your website?

LEWIS: I don't want a website, Emily. *(Pause.)* Look, I know how you feel.

EMILY: Do you?

LEWIS: Yeah, you're disappointed. In me. I've let you down.

EMILY: No, Lewis, I'm scared! Scared for our family. No matter how much we work, we're getting further and further behind. What if Jacob needs to take a break again?

LEWIS: We'll manage.

EMILY: We barely made the rent last month!

LEWIS: But we paid it. Things have a way of working out.

EMILY: Do they? Crossing your fingers is not a plan! This is a huge opportunity.

LEWIS: I know. Believe me, I know. *(Pause.)* It's just—did you see Paul's face? He was not part of the decision.

EMILY: So?

LEWIS: He's my best friend.

EMILY: I'm your wife. Paul throws you work here and there like he's doing you a big favour.

LEWIS: It's not like that.

EMILY: No? A dozen cabinets every month or so for those cheap houses he builds.

LEWIS: He built this house.

EMILY: For himself. It's not even steady work.

LEWIS: At least there's no strings attached.

EMILY: What? Strings? John and Lynne are offering you a real job, for serious money, doing what you love.

LEWIS: Making furniture for rich people.

EMILY: Oh my God. Who else can afford to buy a hand-carved yellow cedar table that takes twenty-four coats of varnish?

LEWIS: The kind of people that stay at these places... helicopters coming in all the time. It changes things.

EMILY: Things changed a long time ago. We can barely afford to live here. Why can't things change for us for once?

LEWIS: How long do we have to stay out here?

EMILY: They want to make it like a surprise.

LEWIS: I don't know if I can handle another surprise.

EMILY: It's dessert, honey. You can handle it.

LEWIS: We could move, you know. Annie's almost done with high school.

EMILY: Are we going back to the Tiny House in the bush fantasy?

LEWIS comes to stand behind EMILY. He kisses her neck.

LEWIS: Self-supporting. Small footprint. I like your new dress.

EMILY: I never should've bought it.

LEWIS: It is a lot of money.

EMILY: A lot of money.

LEWIS: And you don't think it's weird.

EMILY: I think you're worth it. And so do they.

LEWIS: Still...

EMILY: You're overthinking it.

LEWIS: What about trusting my gut?

EMILY: Maybe this time, just trust your wife.

Scene Six: Living Room

JOHN stands in the living room admiring a wolf mask displayed over the fireplace. PAUL enters.

JOHN: Great house, Paul. Who did the fireplace?

PAUL: A local guy. Has his own quarry.

JOHN: And the wolf mask?

PAUL: A gift.

JOHN: Impressive piece. I didn't know you were a collector.

PAUL: I'm not. Lewis gave it to me for my fortieth birthday.

JOHN: Lewis carved this?

PAUL: No. It's Kwakiutl. Done by a master carver who moved up from the coast. Lewis took a class with him.

JOHN: Must be worth something.

PAUL: I think he rewired the guy's studio to help pay for it.

JOHN: Thoughtful present.

PAUL: Always makes me think of Lewis.

JOHN: The lone wolf...

PAUL: No, the grin. It's kinda like the wolf's smiling at some inside joke.

JOHN: Lewis is the real deal. That's for sure. Which is why we want him on the team.

He looks back to the mask.

He could really help us with the locals.

PAUL: *(A beat.)* He'll make up his own mind.

JOHN: But it won't hurt if his best friend helps point him in the right direction. You're lucky. You know, I never had a friend like that growing up. Never had that bond. But then I met Lynne. Kinda took me by surprise. Embarrassing to admit, but I never believed men and women could become friends like that. Always seemed more... transactional to me... you both want something, you fill a need. It was different with Lynne. First time we went out, she refused to let me pay for dinner, right? She was curious... she asked me a lot of questions. She had that confidence... well, *you* know. She made it clear it was *me* she wanted. And God, I sure as hell wanted her. And it grew from there. The intimacy, the trust. It took a while, but now we talk about everything.

He takes a beat, lets it sit.

She's my best friend. Sorta like you and Lewis that way.

PAUL: Right—

JOHN: Thing is, you care about someone that much, they have a certain leverage... in the relationship. And sometimes, that means you'll do anything to keep what you have. You follow me?

PAUL: Look, John—

NICOLE brings the cake out into the living room. She may have overheard the last bit of their conversation.

NICOLE: Okay, you two, cake time, no more business talk. John, would you mind grabbing Lewis and Emily? They're on the terrace.

JOHN: On it, boss.

JOHN salutes her and exits.

NICOLE: Paul, can you help Lynne with the dessert plates?

PAUL: I'm surprised you're putting that cake anywhere near your couch.

NICOLE: It's a special occasion. Plates.

PAUL exits. NICOLE lights the candles on the cake.

JOHN and LEWIS follow EMILY into the living room.

EMILY: Oh my God— It's bigger than our wedding cake!

NICOLE: Oh hold on, hold on... you weren't supposed to see until everyone...

EMILY: It's so beautiful.

JOHN: *(Aside to LEWIS re: EMILY.)* She talk you into it?

LEWIS: We don't talk each other into things. We just talk.

NICOLE: We ordered it from Thomas Haas— I know raspberry chocolate is your favourite—

LYNNE and PAUL enter laughing. PAUL carries the plates, a makeshift blindfold over his eyes.

LYNNE: You're almost there.

PAUL: Don't direct me... I can find my way...

LYNNE: We have a bet.

EMILY: Of course you do.

NICOLE: Paul, what are you doing—?

PAUL: Guys, don't help me, or I lose the bet! I'm almost there... right... putting the plates down here. Am I close? Ow!

PAUL smacks his knee on the sofa. The plates start to fall, but LEWIS catches them.

LEWIS: Got ya!

NICOLE: Oh my God.

JOHN: Nice save, Lewis.

PAUL: I made it!

LYNNE You lose!

EMILY: What did you bet?

PAUL:	Make it to the living room without—	LYNNE:	Make it to the living room without—

LEWIS: Tripping and breaking six plates?

PAUL: No breakage!

LYNNE:	You totally lost the bet, Paul!	EMILY:	Lewis saved you!

JOHN: How much did you bet?

LYNNE: Fifty bucks!

NICOLE: The candles are melting, you guys—

PAUL: Which I won.

LYNNE: Which you did not win!

NICOLE: Come on, everyone, here! I want to get a picture before—

NICOLE wrangles them into position around the cake.

PAUL: Which I almost won.

NICOLE: Lewis. You and Emily in the middle.

Smile, everyone....

They pose for the photo, but JOHN speaks mid-flash, making for an awkward photo.

JOHN: So, are you going to pay up, Paul?

NICOLE: John?!

PAUL: What?

NICOLE: Okay, you two, blow out the candles.

EMILY: Do we get to make a wish?

JOHN: Sounds like you lost the bet. Are you going to pay it?

They all pause over the cake.

PAUL: Yeah sure, I'm going to pay it. *(To LYNNE.)* I owe you fifty bucks. Man, look at that cake!

LYNNE: Don't worry about it— Make a wish, Emily.

JOHN: Can't trust a man who welches on a bet.

LYNNE: John!

NICOLE: The candles—

LEWIS: Paul doesn't welch.

JOHN: Seems to me he still owes *you* five bucks from the Trapper.

PAUL takes out his wallet.

PAUL: Okay, okay, no big deal.

LYNNE: Paul, no!

JOHN: Let the man make good on his bet.

LYNNE: John, really—

JOHN: Take it.

LYNNE takes the money.

JOHN: There. That didn't hurt, did it?

NICOLE: Emily, make a wish and blow out the candles!

EMILY takes LEWIS's hand, makes a wish and blows out the candles. LEWIS kisses her.

PAUSE and then CHEERS.

PAUL/ LYNNE: Speech! Speech!

LYNNE: Come on, Em!

EMILY: I think I've cried enough tonight.

LYNNE: Lewis?

LEWIS: No! No speech, you morons. Ever.

PAUL: No speech from my friend of few words?

NICOLE: *(To PAUL.)* Because you never let him get a word in. Just let them cut the cake.

PAUL: Big piece for me. And hey, no slippage!

LEWIS shakes his head. Puts the knife down.

LEWIS: Actually, I do have something to say. No speech. I just want to say thank you. Thank you to my friends for being here tonight. *(To NICOLE.)* And thank you for the trouble you took to make a really special party for us. *(To PAUL.)* And to you, man, for... for The Meat. And most of all, thank you to my wife for sticking with me for twenty-five years. And John, Lynne, I want to say thank you to you, too, for making me an incredible offer. You know I appreciate it...

Beat. LEWIS grins.

And I accept it.

EMILY: What?!

JOHN steps in to shake LEWIS's hand. General celebration.

ALL: Yay!

JOHN:	Great to hear it, Lewis. It's going to be fun.	LYNNE:	I'm so glad, Lewis!

EMILY: Seriously? Oh my God.

She kisses him.

PAUL: Okay, no more smooching. This calls for cake! Cake! Cake!

LEWIS: You want to do this?

He hands EMILY the knife, but she declines.

EMILY: My hands are shaking. Are you sure about this?

LEWIS: Gotta grow up sometime.

LYNNE: This is fantastic, Lewis! We'll all be working together.

NICOLE: Here, let me do it.

NICOLE takes the knife. Everyone gathers around LEWIS and EMILY, leaving NICOLE alone to cut the cake.

LYNNE: I can't wait to show you the plans. We can all take a drive up to the Orchard tomorrow. I'll walk you through everything.

JOHN raises his glass.

JOHN: Welcome aboard, buddy, you won't regret it. And you know what, I am going to mandate that we take that annual fishing trip you guys missed this year. An official company day off—from now on. The three of us. Or maybe the whole crew. Do it up right. Charter our own fishing boat. My treat.

A look passes between PAUL and LEWIS.

PAUL: Great. Maybe we'll catch something for a change.

PAUL slaps JOHN on the back, winks at LEWIS.

JOHN: Damn right we will.

NICOLE: Paul? Can you maybe help over here?

LYNNE (*To EMILY.*) It's perfect. We'll get to see each other all the time again.

EMILY: Like the old days.

PAUL leans in and pinches NICOLE's ass. She swats his hand away.

PAUL: Looks like you'll be getting your pool, honey. Big piece for me.

NICOLE: Jesus, Paul. Guests of honour first.

LYNNE: Small piece for me.

JOHN: Same. I'm stuffed.

NICOLE: Really?

PAUL: What's wrong with you guys? Here we have this spectacular chocolate raspberry cake, frickin' FedExed from Thomas Haas in Vancouver, and you're going to let it all go to waste? Big piece for me. Bigger!

NICOLE cuts a huge wedge from the cake.

PAUL: Yeah baby, that's more like it.

LYNNE: God, Paul. I don't know where you put it all.

JOHN: The man does have an appetite.

PAUL: I promise, not gonna make a mess on the couch, Mama.

NICOLE looks at him reaching for the cake, then instead of putting it on the plate, she hurls it into PAUL's face.

NICOLE: Big enough for you?!

She storms off into the kitchen. PAUL stands there dumbfounded, wiping away the cake and frosting to stunned silence.

JOHN: Bamboo napkin?

PAUL follows NICOLE.

Scene Seven: Kitchen

NICOLE moves around the kitchen in a fury, preparing a tray for coffee, cups, cream, sugar, etc. PAUL enters. He wipes his face and clothes off with a dish towel.

PAUL: Jesus, Nic, what the hell was that? Are you going to talk to me? Honey, come on, please, what is it?

NICOLE: Don't "honey" me. And don't you ever pinch me on the ass in front of your friends again! I'm not your fucking property.

PAUL: Is that what this is? Okay, okay, I'm sorry. Just stop.

NICOLE: You really don't see it, do you?!

PAUL: What?!

NICOLE: You're like a greedy little kid... stuffing your face, kowtowing to John!

PAUL: Keep your voice down.

NICOLE: There you go—better keep our voices down. Wouldn't want John thinking anything was wrong. Where's your dignity, for God's sake!

PAUL: My dignity? You just threw a fucking piece of cake in my face. Dignity does not seem to be a major concern at the moment.

NICOLE: That's all you care about! Don't want me to jeopardize your precious deal, embarrass your friends—

PAUL: It's *our* deal, Nicole. We need this. You know that.

NICOLE: Then stop pretending it's all about *me* wanting a stupid swimming pool.

PAUL: I was joking! Christ, I thought you were on board with this.

NICOLE: Not if we all have to get on John's fucking boat, I'm not!

NICOLE accidentally knocks a plate to the floor. It shatters. She falls to her knees to pick it up.

PAUL: Jesus, are we on about the goddamn boat thing again?

NICOLE: You don't see it. He's already taking control. How do you think Lewis feels about his new fishing partner?

PAUL stoops down to help her.

PAUL: Stop. You'll cut yourself. Lewis took the job. He knows what he's getting into.

NICOLE: All you're thinking about is the money.

PAUL: Of course I'm thinking about the money. Somebody has to!

NICOLE: Well, it's not very attractive.

PAUL sits back on his heels.

PAUL: You know, I think John is right about you.

NICOLE: What?

PAUL: You hate that we need this. You want to stand on your environmental principles or whatever the fuck it was you were talking about tonight *and* you want the swimming pool. And it drives you crazy. Just admit it! You want to get on the boat, you just don't want anybody to see you doing it.

NICOLE: Oh my God! What I want is for you to stand up for me!

PAUL: Stand up for you?

NICOLE: When someone dismisses me the way he did. Talks to me that way. I want you to SAY something.

PAUL: You'd bite my head off if I spoke for you—

NICOLE: Not speak for me—defend me. Act like you respect my feelings. He walks all over you.

PAUL: So?

NICOLE: So?!

PAUL: How do you think all this gets paid for?

PAUL slaps the countertop.

NICOLE: I know how it gets paid for.

PAUL: Do you? Then you know that we're fucking leveraged up to our necks. This, this, this, this, that! *(He slaps the wall, the floor, the table, in a fury.)* It's all leveraged against this one deal! This deal that *you* thought was such a great idea in Mexico. "The next level for us," you said. *(He points at her.)* It was *your* fucking idea! "Talk to Lynne about developing it together, Paul." So here we are, goin' to the next level, babe! Except, I'm bleeding out here. And you're making it worse, because you won't let up on John. Listen to me, if it makes John happy to compromise my "dignity," as you call it, then I'm okay with it. Because it's the only way we get back on our feet again. I don't know what game he's playing, and I don't really care. All I know is I need to play along with it. And so do you. That's how you get to save the world and pay for that fancy chandelier. So stop being such a hypocrite and get on the goddamn boat!

Beat.

NICOLE: Did you sleep with her?

PAUL: What?

NICOLE: Lynne.

PAUL: What are you talking about?

NICOLE: In Mexico?

PAUL: We had dinner. You didn't want to come. We went for a drive to talk. I told you.

NICOLE: We used to talk.

PAUL: Look, we cannot do this right now.

NICOLE: I'm not crazy.

PAUL: You're doing this to yourself, Nicole.

NICOLE: Paul?

PAUL: I did not sleep with her. Are you coming?

NICOLE doesn't move. PAUL picks up the tray with the coffee and heads back to the living room. NICOLE locates a hidden pack of cigarettes and exits to the terrace.

Scene Eight: Living Room

Uncomfortable silence. Only LEWIS eats cake.

LEWIS: Good cake.

EMILY: It's the icing.

PAUL enters with the coffee. They all stand up.

PAUL: Wow. Do I get a military salute, too?

JOHN: Depends, did you win the battle?

PAUL: I'm sorry about that—

LYNNE: Is she... everything, okay?

PAUL: She'll be fine.

EMILY: You still have some... cake... in your hair.

PAUL swipes at his hair. Licks his finger.

PAUL: And damn fine cake it is. Who wants coffee?

EMILY: Maybe I should go see—

PAUL: Come on, it's your party. She'll be back.

JOHN: Can't have your cake and throw it too, right?

EMILY catches LEWIS's eye and nods towards the terrace.

LEWIS: I'll go.

LEWIS exits to the terrace.

JOHN: I need to make a phone call, if that's okay?

PAUL: Sure. Why don't I show you guys your room? And then we can regroup.

LYNNE: *(To EMILY.)* We'll be right back.

EMILY: I'm not going anywhere.

JOHN: There's some of the cuvée left if you get thirsty.

JOHN and LYNNE follow PAUL out. EMILY drinks her wine.

Scene Nine: Terrace

NICOLE stands on the terrace smoking. LEWIS joins her. They stand for a moment before LEWIS speaks.

LEWIS: I didn't know you smoked.

NICOLE: Only when I want to kill my husband. I'm sorry, I didn't mean to ruin the party.

LEWIS: I got a job. Em's ecstatic. We're good.

NICOLE: I'm happy for you guys. Really. God, I hate the taste of these things.

LEWIS: It's the trade-off for stuffing your feelings.

NICOLE: Well, then... I think we better keep my feelings firmly stuffed for the rest of the night.

Why did you take the job?

LEWIS: We need the money.

NICOLE: But it doesn't feel right to you... I can tell.

LEWIS: I took it for my family. I can live with that.

NICOLE: Paul said some things in the kitchen...

LEWIS: People say things when they're angry.

NICOLE: The things he said... I think he might be right. I question myself all the time... I want things, then I feel guilty for wanting them. I try to do the right thing, but at the same time, I feel like I'm being a self-entitled bitch... It's like I can't trust my instincts anymore.

LEWIS: You know, Em and I had a big argument that day I found her... the wolf. About Jacob, money... all of it. I had no idea what to do. I took off in my truck. Needed to clear my head. Hiked all the way up past the snow line on the mountain. *(Pause.)* I heard the keening first... thought maybe it was a dog who'd gotten lost. Except I knew there was an old trapline up there... so I kept going towards the sound. That's when I saw her. Her foreleg was caught in the clamp of a leg-hold trap... mangled and all chewed up where she'd tried to get free... lying on her side, like she'd been wrestling with it for a long time, and she'd finally given up. She lifted her head when she saw me—tried growling, but I could tell her heart wasn't in it. There was a broken tree branch near the trap... and I...

NICOLE: You put her out of her misery.

LEWIS: *(Nods.)* I was going to leave... but then I heard this low snarling. I thought somehow she was still alive, but it wasn't her, it was a huge male standing in the trees about twenty feet away, watching me, his teeth bared. Probably her mate. He started moving towards me. I still had the branch in my hand... I thought of running, but I knew I didn't stand a chance, so I backed off a little, faced him. He came as far as the trap, watching me the whole time. I thought he was going to lunge, but instead, he lowered his head to her body and he nuzzled her, gently, with his snout, his eyes never leaving me. Then, he raised his head, and he howled. The sound of it... it cut straight through me, into some place I didn't even know was there. And from way off in the woods came another howl... and another. And that wolf looked at me with those... eyes, then he was gone. I stood there with all that blood on the snow... and I swear to God, I just lost it. I didn't know what to do... about Jacob, work, any of it. Why did I end up there? I don't know. But I knew it was all connected somehow. And I knew what to do right then.

NICOLE: So you brought her home.

LEWIS: I couldn't leave her there... for the trapper. I needed to pay attention in some way. She deserved that much.

NICOLE: She did.

LEWIS puts his hand on hers.

LEWIS: You do know what's right. I know you do, Nicole.

Impulsively, NICOLE kisses LEWIS.

Hey—What are you doing?

NICOLE: I thought—

LEWIS: No, you're confused—

NICOLE: But you said—

LEWIS: You got it wrong—

NICOLE: Lewis—

LEWIS: —It's okay, I need to go back inside.

LEWIS starts heading back in.

NICOLE: Lewis, wait—

LEWIS exits. NICOLE watches him go.

I'm sorry...

Scene Ten: Living Room

EMILY sits on the living room couch. The container of red paint rests against her leg as she dips her brush in and finishes painting "Love" on her rock. LYNNE enters.

LYNNE: There she is. What are you doing?

EMILY: Painting our rocks.

EMILY shows her the rock and picks up another.

LYNNE: Very nice.

EMILY: I think "compromise" has way too many letters. For a rock.

LYNNE: Your party seems to have been hijacked.

EMILY: I don't know that it was ever our party.

LYNNE: Is she still out there?

EMILY: I'm sure Lewis will be able to console her.

LYNNE picks up a brush and rock.

LYNNE: Why do you say it like that?

EMILY: Come on, she's always had a thing for him.

LYNNE: Really. That doesn't bother you?

EMILY: God no. It's funny the things people get upset about. When they have everything they want.

LYNNE: You know, I feel like I need to apologize.

EMILY: Why?

LYNNE: I haven't been much of a friend lately. I didn't even know you'd moved out to the lake.

EMILY: It's no big deal. Like I said, we're not even on the water.

LYNNE: But it's nice, right? Close to the school.

EMILY: Actually, it's drafty. And it's small. And its overpriced. And it doesn't matter. Because "we have each other. And that's what counts." Right?

LYNNE: But you're lucky, Em. What you've done with your family. That is what counts.

EMILY: I know what I have, Lynne. I may not know the price of that chandelier. But I do know the value of things. You don't need to patronize me.

LYNNE: I wasn't—

EMILY: Look, I can be grateful and disappointed at the same time. I'm complicated like that.

LYNNE: *(Laughs.)* I've missed you, Em.

EMILY: Me too.

They paint.

LYNNE: I know it doesn't look that way, but I didn't get everything I want.

EMILY: I know. You would have been a great mom. Or at least you'd have hired a great nanny.

LYNNE: I still have that little plastic grizzly key chain Lewis gave me that night at The Trapper.

EMILY: He wanted to cheer you up. We all did.

LYNNE: I couldn't have gone through all that without you. You were really there for me.

EMILY: Do you ever ...

LYNNE: Regret it? I was too young. I couldn't have kept it. And with Paul... no. He's not Lewis. I made the right choice.

EMILY: I guess we both did.

LYNNE: I was hoping I'd get a second chance. With John.

EMILY: We put Jacob in a drawer when he was born. That was his nursery. Sometimes I wanted to close it. The drawer. With him in it. When he cried. The colic.

LYNNE: It hasn't been an easy road with Jacob, has it?

EMILY: No. My boy.

Beat.

LYNNE: Something happened down in Mexico. With Paul.

EMILY: Okay...

LYNNE: It was a total mistake. Something about being there with him... Talking about the Orchard. It brought back... I thought I could... I can't believe it happened. I wish it hadn't.

EMILY: But it did.

LYNNE: I told John. I had to. We worked through it. In some ways our relationship is stronger because of it. We've moved on. That was our deal. Paul doesn't even know that I told him.

EMILY: Then why tell me?

LYNNE: I care what you think—

EMILY: Why?

LYNNE: You're a good person. My best friend. I used to tell you everything.

EMILY: And now, you hardly even talk to me.

LYNNE: I'm talking to you now. I'm trying to tell you something important—

EMILY: Don't tell me! Okay, Lynne? Don't confide. Don't get it off your chest and leave it with me. Okay?

LYNNE: What—?

EMILY: We're not those girls in the Orchard. We can't go back there.

LYNNE: I just wanted to talk to you—

EMILY: Because you feel guilty! You did something wrong. Or you think you did. And you want to feel better. So you dump it on me. You're confessing to me because at the end of the day it *doesn't* matter to you what I think anymore. Or how I feel. If it did, you'd know where I live. And how my son is doing. If it actually mattered to you what I think, we'd still be friends.

LYNNE: That's not fair.

EMILY: You know, sometimes I think it's stupid to even worry about what's right or wrong. What's the point? Look at the world... how people act. Everyone's just doing what they want anyway. I don't even know how any of it works anymore.

LYNNE: Maybe you should slow down on the wine, Em.

EMILY: Yeah, maybe.

LYNNE gets up from the couch, knocking EMILY's arm and spilling the red paint onto the white sofa.

EMILY: Oh my God! No! The paint!

LYNNE: What did you do?

EMILY: Me? You bumped me— never mind, hand me those napkins.

LYNNE hands her the napkins. EMILY wipes at the growing stain on the couch, her hands covered in red paint.

LYNNE: Don't spread it! I'll get a towel.

EMILY: Oh no! Hurry!

LYNNE goes for the towel.

LEWIS enters. For a moment he is stunned by what he sees: the injured wolf, the blood, the snow, and then: EMILY on her knees, pawing with her red hands at a bloody stain on the couch.

LEWIS snaps out of it and runs to kneel by EMILY.

LEWIS: Jesus! Emily? Are you okay?

EMILY: I didn't mean to—

LEWIS: Are you hurt?

EMILY: What—? No!

LEWIS: You're bleeding.

EMILY: It's the paint! Help, Lewis, it's spreading.

LEWIS gets up as LYNNE enters with soda water and a towel, passes it to LEWIS.

PAUL enters.

LYNNE: Here. Do the soda first.

PAUL: Okay, let's get this party—Jesus Christ! What happened?

<table>
<tr><td>EMILY:</td><td>Paul, I'm sorry. I was just—</td><td>LYNNE:</td><td>It was an accident.</td></tr>
</table>

PAUL pushes EMILY out of the way.

PAUL: Stop! You're making it worse. Here, give me that!

PAUL gets down on his knees to start rubbing at the stain.

How the hell—?

JOHN enters on his phone.

JOHN: Monday's great. Hey, I gotta let you go—

EMILY: I'm so sorry!

PAUL: Jesus Christ, Emily, drink much!

LEWIS: Easy, Paul.

PAUL: You take it easy!

LYNNE: You'll have to get it cleaned.

LEWIS: We'll pay for it.

PAUL: Really? We're gonna take it out of your first paycheque?

JOHN: Stop it, Paul! It's just a couch, right?

JOHN stands over PAUL. NICOLE enters from the terrace.

NICOLE: Oh, no. What happened—

PAUL: *(To NICOLE.)* Emily spilled— I'm trying to—

EMILY: I just wanted to paint my rock—I'm so sorry, Nicole.

NICOLE: It's okay, it's okay.

JOHN: Accidents happen.

PAUL: This isn't fucking working.

NICOLE: It was a silly idea anyway. Paul, get off the floor.

PAUL starts to get up off his hands and knees, but JOHN puts his foot down on PAUL's hand, pinning it to the floor and keeping PAUL in a submissive position.

JOHN: I think you need to apologize.

PAUL: Ow! Hey, man—

JOHN: To Emily.

PAUL: What are you—?

EMILY: It's okay. It was my fault, I—

PAUL: My hand—

JOHN: You overstepped, Paul.

LYNNE: John—

LEWIS: Stop it, John.

PAUL: Goddamnit, John. This isn't funny.

JOHN: Tell Emily you're sorry.

LEWIS: I think we get the point—

LYNNE: John, that's enough.

JOHN: *(To LYNNE.)* You don't get a say in this.

JOHN steps harder.

PAUL: Jesus—okay, okay! I'm sorry, Emily.

JOHN: For what?

PAUL: For yelling. Saying you drink too much?

EMILY: It's okay, Paul. *(To JOHN.)* John, I'm okay!

JOHN: And what else? Let's clear the air while you're down there.

LEWIS: Get the fuck off him!

LEWIS lunges towards JOHN. PAUL puts his free hand up to stop him.

PAUL: It's okay, Lewis.

NICOLE: Let him finish.

JOHN lifts his foot off PAUL's hand, but PAUL stays on his knees.

LYNNE: John, please.

JOHN: No. You created this mess. I'm trying to clean it up. Get it out in the open. He apologizes. And I forgive. Then we can all move forward. Like you wanted.

PAUL: Look, I didn't mean to—

JOHN completely loses it.

JOHN: Don't you dare, you sonofabitch! And don't you fucking look at her! That's my wife. I told you, we tell each other everything. Everything. I trusted her. And you fucking broke that trust!

PAUL drops his head, submitting completely.

PAUL: I'm sorry! I'm sorry, John.

JOHN: For what?

PAUL: For what happened in Mexico.

JOHN: With my wife.

PAUL: With your wife.

JOHN: I don't think Nicole heard you.

PAUL: Oh fuck, Nicole, I am so sorry. Fuck.

JOHN: Get up.

PAUL gets to his feet, moves off to the side of the room, not meeting anyone's eyes.

Nobody moves.

An uncomfortably long pause.

NICOLE: Well...at the very least, I think we've cleared the air here.

They all turn and look at NICOLE.

LYNNE: Nicole, I—

NICOLE stops her with a hand.

NICOLE: It's okay. I think John just wanted to make sure we're all on the same boat here. Right, John? That we understand there are certain rules when people work together. And we all do want to work together, don't we, Lynne?

LYNNE: Yes... that's all I ever wanted. To be with my friends.

NICOLE: And friendship is what matters. So, I think we're good.

LEWIS: What the hell?

NICOLE: People make mistakes, Lewis. We can move on now. That's what we all want. To move on. Right, John?

JOHN takes his cue from NICOLE.

JOHN: Paul, look, I'm... that was Artie I called. He's ready to sign. It's all taken care of.

NICOLE: That's great. Isn't it, Paul?

PAUL: *(Quietly.)* Great.

NICOLE: Well, I don't know about everyone else, but I could certainly use a glass of wine. John, would you...?

JOHN fills wineglasses. The others are still a little dumbfounded.

LEWIS: *(To NICOLE.)* Are you really okay with this?

NICOLE: Hey, you know me, Lewis, I'm just in it for the swimming pool.

JOHN hands her a glass of wine.

NICOLE: Thank you. So here we are. A toast. To friends working together—

Suddenly the smoke alarm goes off. EMILY jumps. They all stand there as the piercing sound continues.

Paul, go turn it off.

PAUL starts to say something but then nods and leaves to turn off the smoke alarm. They wait.

They're so sensitive—

EMILY: —Shouldn't we—?

NICOLE: It's just the smoke from the fires...

LYNNE: Maybe you need a Hepa filter?

The alarm sound stops.

NICOLE: Everything's fine. That's better.

PAUL returns.

JOHN: Look, I'd like to propose a toast of my own. If that's okay? I'm sorry about all the... drama. But Nicole's right, we all know what's important here.

He puts an arm around LYNNE.

Creating a very special place, with special people. What could be better?

JOHN raises his glass. NICOLE and LYNNE follow, LEWIS and EMILY a little more tentatively. Finally, PAUL does, too.

Money's in place, a beautiful piece of land, wonderful designer, and an excellent craftsman to round out the team. Lewis talks to a few of his buddies, and I predict it's smooth sailing.

LEWIS lowers his glass.

LEWIS: My buddies?

JOHN: Your friends... on the Rez... maybe you want a few of them on your team. You know, get 'em to create some buzz about the project...so we get everybody on board with this. Stem any blowback.

LEWIS: You mean from the Tribe. You're talking about the permits...

JOHN: It's all about relationships, Lewis.

LEWIS: I don't know, John. Doesn't feel right to me.

JOHN: Funny. Talking to Marcel about getting Jacob that job felt right to me.

LEWIS: Jacob got himself that job. It's not the same thing.

JOHN: You sure about that? *(Pause.)* What? You think I'm paying you two-hundred-and-fifty-thousand dollars a year just to build some cabinets? One of Paul's guys could do that. C'mon, relationships are worth something. Especially when everybody benefits.

LEWIS: I don't use my friends that way.

JOHN: You're saying you don't want to throw your friends an opportunity? Or are you saying you don't believe in what we're doing at the Orchard?

LEWIS: I'm saying I don't want to use my friends that way.

JOHN: Even if you're getting paid a shitload of money to do it? Even when it's a good thing?

LEWIS: I don't know if it's a good thing.

JOHN: Right. See, I think you *do* know, Lewis. And that's why you don't want to talk to your buddies. Maybe you're the one who isn't being honest. And I gotta tell you, if you don't believe in what we're doing here, that's gonna be a problem.

LEWIS meets EMILY'S eyes. She nods. He takes the cheque from his pocket and gives it to JOHN.

LEWIS: You're right, John, this isn't going to work.

JOHN: *(Shrugs.)* Suit yourself.

JOHN takes the cheque.

LYNNE: We can figure this out—

EMILY: I think we need to go home.

LYNNE: What? No! It's your party.

PAUL is looking at the floor.

EMILY: I just need my purse.

NICOLE: Can I wrap up some cake for you?

PAUL: I'll see you guys out.

LEWIS: We're good.

PAUL hands EMILY her purse.

PAUL: *(Softly.)* You still love me, Em?

EMILY: Always, Paul.

EMILY kisses him on the cheek.

NICOLE: And don't you worry about that couch!

EMILY: Right. Thanks.

LYNNE Love you guys.

JOHN: Drive safe.

NICOLE: *(Calling after them.)* Happy anniversary!

EMILY and LEWIS exit.

Beat.

What are you doing over there, Paul?

PAUL: Just making sure they get out okay.

PAUL stands apart from the others. LYNNE turns to study the couch.

LYNNE: You know... I could have my upholsterer make an identical piece. He's really good. You won't be able to tell the difference. Like it never happened.

NICOLE: Maybe we should just think about replacing it.

LYNNE: Well... I do have this fabulous new supplier. Imports beautiful pieces direct from Milan. We could make a day of it in the city. If you want... me and you?

NICOLE: I am coming down to see my mom next week...

LYNNE: That's perfect.

JOHN: Problem solved. *(Beat.)* Too bad about those two.

NICOLE: Well, you try and help people, right? Paul? Come back here and join the party. There's more cake.

PAUL: No, thanks. I'm full.

PAUL stays by the window looking out after his friends.

Scene Eleven: Moonlight

EMILY and LEWIS stand looking at the moon.

LEWIS: Smoke's clearing a little. Full moon.

EMILY: Makes you feel like howling, doesn't it?

LEWIS: You know, they don't actually do that. Howl at the moon. People just made that up.

EMILY: So what are they howling at?

LEWIS: They're talking. To each other.

EMILY: What are they saying?

LEWIS pauses.

LEWIS: They're saying, "I'm here. Can you hear me? I'm right here."

Lights down on EMILY and LEWIS.

PAUL remains alone at the window.

The fire burns.

End of play.